Other Books by tjjohnson

The Genesis Men, Adam & Sons, 2009; Xlibris
The Genesis Men, Noah & Sons, 2012; AuthorHouse
The Genesis Men, Abraham & Sons, 2015; AuthorHouse

Chapter & Verse, Crosswords & Other Puzzles,
Genesis Book One, 2008; Xulon Press

Chapter & Verse, Crosswords & Other Puzzles,
Genesis Book Two, 2009; AuthorHouse

Chapter & Verse, Crosswords & Other Puzzles,
Verse Variety, 2011; AuthorHouse

THE GENESIS MEN, JACOB & SONS, TWELVE TRIBES

tjjohnson

authorHOUSE®

AuthorHouse™
1663 Liberty Drive
Bloomington, IN 47403
www.authorhouse.com
Phone: 1 (800) 839-8640

Published by AuthorHouse 03/07/2018

ISBN: 978-1-5462-0694-1 (sc)
ISBN: 978-1-5462-0693-4 (e)

Print information available on the last page.

Any people depicted in stock imagery provided by Thinkstock are models, and such images are being used for illustrative purposes only. Certain stock imagery © Thinkstock.

This book is printed on acid-free paper.

Because of the dynamic nature of the Internet, any web addresses or links contained in this book may have changed since publication and may no longer be valid. The views expressed in this work are solely those of the author and do not necessarily reflect the views of the publisher, and the publisher hereby disclaims any responsibility for them.

Unless otherwise indicated, Biblical information taken from The King James Version of the Holy Bible, copyright ©1988 by Liberty University.

My Sincere Appreciation
To Friends and Family and Associates
Who Offered Encouragement,
Valuable Feedback,
And Suggestions
That
Intensified My Thoughts
And
Enhanced This Book's Content
And Presentation.

Edited by:
Pamela Gohlke
Michael Johnson
Jo Linda Johnson

In Searching to Know Thyself,
Thou Must Know Thy History;
So, Thou Can Absorb
That Where Thou Art Treading,
Thine Ancestors Have Already Trod.

tjjohnson

~ Contents ~

~ Reference Tables & Maps ~

For ease in following tables:
Shem labeled (I)
Ham labeled (II)
Japheth labeled (III

~ FOREWORD ~

This is the fourth and final book of *The Genesis Men* Bible Study Series which concentrates on the sons of Jacob, one of a trio of forefathers mentioned throughout the Bible. First, Abraham; then Isaac; and then Jacob, the father of twelve sons destined to become the Twelve Tribes of Israel, and later—the nation of Israel.

Rather than an extensive history of the tribes, you will find these pages a limited summary. Everything concerning the Israeli tribes cannot possibly be covered in this book. A great deal of the Old Testament centers around the tribes and their history. Several chapters outline their migration, and the subsequent commands from the LORD who arranged their release from Egypt. These guidelines were meant to direct their everyday lives, encouraging them to be faithful to their God, to live accordingly, and set an example for others to embrace.

When Israel departed Egypt, God fought the Egyptian warriors, and parted the Red Sea—Reed Sea.[1] The Tribes had many battles ahead of them in order to live in the land which God told their forefathers was theirs to take. They had to fight to take possession when they reached Canaan, and they had to fight to keep possession and remain in their land. They won battles when they followed God's commands; they lost battles when they ignored God's commands. Their fight continues to this day, even after centuries have past.

The primary aim of this writing is to capture highlights of each tribe, especially their tribal heroes and the influence on their era. Hopefully, the lesson questions will inspire curiosity beyond obvious information and prompt examination of cross references. Coordination of segmented information helps frame a better understanding of the story being told.

These studies are designed for individual or group. Group study may require splitting chapters to fit into a particular time period. A few lessons may be completed in an hour; others may require longer. My belief is that time, discussion, and understanding are paramount considerations in any Bible study. I'm sure you will structure adaptation to your unique needs.

~ INTRODUCTION ~

The history and activity of the tribes of Israel continue throughout the Bible, although covered in depth in the Old Testament. Moses tells their story during his time of leadership from Egypt to their inheritance—the land of Canaan, according to God's promises. Before Moses, there was Abraham, Isaac, and Jacob. (Gen 13:12, 14-17:18; 48:2-4; 1Chr 16:18; Ps 105:6-11).

God chose Moses as a leader of His special people, guiding Moses in everything he did, including the history that he recorded. That was the Torah, the first five books of the Old Testament, and the Jewish written law. God was insistent and detailed in training Moses, and Moses was careful to lead Israel accordingly. (Ex 17:14; 33:19; 34:1; 34:27; Deu 17:18; 27:3, 8; 31:19).

After the books of Moses, comes Joshua, the prophets, and kings, (Is 30:8; Jer 30:2; 36:2; Ez 43:11; Hab 2:2). In the New Testament are the scribes and apostles. The following references offer some insight and verification: (Jhn 1:45; Acts 25:26; 1Cor 4:14; 2Cor 1:13 & 9:1; Gal 1:20; Phil 3:1; Heb 8:10; 2Pet 3:1; 1Jo 2:1; 1Jo 2:7; Jud 1:3; Revelation (Rev) 1:11, 19; Rev 2:1, 8, 12, 18; 3:1, 7, 12, 14; 14:13; 19:9, 21:5).

Why did God choose Israel, and not another nation? There are many things that are not intended for us to know, at the present. So much so that according to John there is not enough space in the Bible, nor in the entire world, to write about them all. God gave us the answers He wanted us to know; all other things are considered His to know. As for Israel, Jehovah God chose whomever He would chose. His decision. His plan. (John 21:25; Deu 29:29; Ex 6:7; Lev 26:12; Jer 7:23; Dan 2:22).

During their lifetime, both Jacob and Moses spoke blessings into the lives of each tribal leader. These coveted words were traditionally given when a father—or leader in the case of Moses—was about to join his ancestors. Jacob blessed his sons, his original twelve, and the two sons of Joseph. Moses blessed the chief of each tribe just before his demise. (See: Gen 48:15, 21-22; Deu 33).

Several times in the lives of Israel, a younger son was blessed above the eldest son. First Abraham's son Isaac inherited the promise of the land, not Ishmael. God's covenant and prophecy was for the son of Abraham and Sarah, not Abraham and Hagar, (Gen 16:15; 17:15-21). Isaac's son Esau was born before his twin brother Jacob. Nevertheless, Jacob was designated to receive the blessing of the LORD's promise before either he or Esau was born. And, God's covenant was reconfirmed to Jacob in the words of his father, by the words of the LORD, (Gen 28:1, 3-4; 13-15).

Further, Jacob negotiated for the first-born blessing of his brother during a time when Esau was extremely hungry, and careless, to the extent that he traded his birthright to Jacob for a serving of pottage, or stew, (Gen 25:29-34). Jacob's firstborn, Reuben, forfeited his rights when he dishonored his privileges as ruler of the household while his father was away. His younger brother Joseph received the blessings instead, first from his father, and then from Moses. (Gen 48:21-22; 49:22-26; Deu 33:13-17).

Another example of a younger son blessed above an older brother is seen in the case of Joseph's sons. Jacob adopted his grandsons and blessed them first, before he blessed his other sons, (Gen 48:5-22; 1Chr 5:1). One might think that two more sons would result in fourteen tribes, not twelve. But, in any listing of the tribes, there are always twelve names. Most often, the tribe of Levi is omitted, as their inheritance was their service unto the LORD. To account for the sons of Joseph, either his name appears in the list, or the name of one of his sons—Ephraim or Manasseh.

One blessing skipped not one brother, nor ten brothers—as seen with Joseph over Reuben—but seven brothers! This blessing was made known when God instructed the prophet Samuel to appoint a son of Jesse as the next king of Israel. Jesse presented seven of his sons to Samuel before he remembered his son David, who was tending the flock. God chose this younger son above all his older brothers. God chooses whom HE will, to fulfill His purposes, when HE desires it. (Gen 48:5-20; 1Sam 16:1, 10-13).

Many years after Israel occupied their new land; after there were kings established in Israel; after the reign of King David, and his son, King Solomon, there was a major disagreement about who should be king in Israel. Even during King David's lifetime, his very own son, Absalom, lobbied and usurped his father's role as king, (2 Sam 15-18). According to God's words through Jacob, kings of Israel were destined to originate from the line of Judah, (Gen 49:8-12). That is, except King Saul, who was a son of Benjamin; and the line of kings which began with Jeroboam, one of Solomon's servants; and a son of Ephraim. (1 Sam 9:1-17; 1 Kings (Ki) 11:1-13, 26-40; 12:20).

During that time, the families were separated into two distinct kingdoms. Most lived in the Northern part of their lands, which included ten tribes. They were known as the Northern Kingdom, and designated as Israel. The smaller kingdom remained in Judah of the south, known as the Southern Kingdom. They were known as the house of Judah, and consisted of the tribes of Judah and of Benjamin, initially, (1Ki 12:20-15:30).

The information of this book offers only a sketch of what has previously been written of Israel. Hopefully, this bit of history, your insights, and discussions that result from your study, will help you understand the Word of God more fully. And create within you an insatiable desire for more.

Suggested Research Materials:

Online Bibles and other research materials; Bible Dictionaries, Histories, Encyclopedias, Commentaries; Strong's Concordance Information;

Hebrew and Greek Translations; and Roget's Thesaurus.

[1] www.blueletterbible.org (Tools, Interlinear Tab, Exodus 10:19)
All Bible references used in this book are from The King James Study Bible.

~ JACOB / ISRAEL ~

Jacob,
Son of Isaac,
Son of Abraham,
Brother of Esau,
And Heir of God.

Jacob left his homeland
as his grandfather had before him.
Jacob was sneakily unfair
to his brother Esau,
who determined to kill Jacob
When their father died.

Rebekah, their mother,
convinced Jacob to run for his life.
His father agreed that Jacob flee
to Rebekah's brother, Laban.
So, Jacob traveled to the land
of his mother's kin:
A Syrian, of Padan-aram.

Jacob found Rachel there,
Along with her sister, Leah,
the daughters of Laban, his Uncle.
He married both and fathered twelve sons.
God later changed Jacob's name to *Israel,*
(after a struggle) and likened him to a prince,
who possessed power with God and men.
Arrangement by tjjohnson
(From Genesis 25:19-32:28)

~ 1 ~

~The ForeFathers ~
Abraham, Isaac, and Jacob

Background Scriptures:
Genesis 12:1-7; 13:12-17; 15:1-7; 17:1-8;
21, 25, 26, 28, 32, & 35

"And Jacob dreamed…And, behold the LORD…said, I am the Lord God of Abraham thy father, and the God of Isaac:… and in thee, and in thy seed, shall all the families of the earth be blessed." (Gen 28:13-14, KJV).

Abraham, Isaac, and Jacob—the trilogy of ancestors whom God declared to fulfill his blessings, and the covenant He made with them, beginning with Abraham. God prophesied that Abram would become 'the father of many nations,' (Gen 17:4).

The first promise made to Abraham concerning his descendants is in Genesis, (Gen)12:1-3. Later it is repeated in chapter 13:14-18; in chapter 15:1-7; and in chapter 17:1-8. In Gen 17:15-22, God confirmed that Isaac, who had not yet been born, would be the one in whom He would establish His covenant, and continue His promise made to Abraham. The oath God had sworn to Abraham was confirmed with Isaac in chapter twenty-six. In chapter twenty-eight, God appeared to Jacob in a dream reaffirming the pledge given to his father and his grandfather.

Jacob was born a twin. The names of Jacob and his older brother Esau give clues to their character. Jacob translates as heel holder, supplanter, and one with devious tendencies.[1] Esau translates as hairy and red, (Gen 25:25-26). Jacob was a favorite of his mother; Esau pleased his father.

Jacob's name was later changed to Israel. This happened during the journey back home after living in the land of his father-in-law for twenty years. As he neared his homeland, he began to dread the unavoidable reunion with Esau. One night, Jacob had a predestined wrestling match with an angel. This angel is referred to as *a man* in scripture, but Jacob later described him as God.

During that struggle, the wrestling intensified and the *man* touched the hollow of Jacob's thigh. That powerful touch caused Jacob's thigh to become displaced out of joint, and his muscle shrank. This explains the reason why the Israelite people do not eat of the thigh muscle, (Gen 32:24-32). Afterward, when the *God Angel* talked with Jacob, *He* changed Jacob's name to Israel.

Many years later, when there was a famine in the land, Jacob relocated his family to Egypt, leaving Canaan to join Joseph. At that time sixty-six sons and daughters of Jacob's family came with him to Egypt—their wives were not counted. Joseph and his two sons were already living in Egypt, which made the total of Jacob's seed to be sixty-nine people. Counting Jacob, his family in Egypt was seventy people, (Gen 46). Before his death, Jacob blessed his sons, (Gen 49). Many, many, years later, Moses also blessed Jacob's sons. These blessings actually foretold the life paths the tribes would take; a prophecy. From that time forward, Jacob's sons were known as the *Twelve Tribes of Israel*.

This is the story of their lives and their contributions to humanity. Even unto the throne of God.

[1] *www.blueletterbible.org*

Lesson Discussion: Various Scriptures
Read Genesis 12:1-2 & 7; 15:17-18; 17:1-8 and 15-22
1. Explain the meaning of the word *covenant*.

2. Discuss the covenant God made with Abram to be passed on to His chosen heirs.

3. God changed Abram's name to Abraham in Gen 17:5. Even though we can never know the mind of God, discuss possible reasons for:
a). The name change:

b). That specific time:

Read Genesis 16:11-15; 17:15-21; 25:29-34; 26:24-25; 27:24-40; 28:10-22

4. In naming blessings, an older son was sometimes bypassed in favor of a younger son. Discuss the men below and their blessings.

a). Isaac and Ishmael.

b). Jacob and Esau.

5. Biblical names imply significant information about one's character. Give translation, and discuss what is revealed about these men.

a). Ishmael

b). Isaac

c). Esau

d). Jacob

e). Israel

6. Jacob dreamed of a ladder where angels went back and forth from heaven to earth. The LORD stood above it and spoke to Jacob. Discuss this dream.

7. Genesis 28:17 tells us that Jacob was afraid of the dreadful place he saw in his dream. Discuss the following as interpreted in context of scripture:
a). Afraid

b). Fear

c). Dreadful

d). House of God

e). Gate of Heaven

8. Jacob made a vow to God in Gen 28:20-22. Explain the promise made. What is the significance of his vow?

9a. Why was the wrestling match special to Jacob in Gen 32:24-32?

9b. What was the outcome of that match?

9c. How is it determined whether this was an angel, or God himself?

Read Genesis 1:1-2; 1:26; 2:4

10. The very first use of God is in Gen 1:1. Research the meaning of God in this verse, and explain. See online information or hardcopy of Strong's Concordance to find the word, and annotate the number linked with it. Old Testament words are translated in Hebrew; NT is in Greek.

11a. Compare the words '*let us,* and *our'* in verse 26 with *God* of verse one. Why are these words considered plural? Use Biblical research tools.

11b. How and where is the Spirit introduced in Genesis?

12. The word *LORD* in all caps is used exclusively in the Old Testament, (KJV). First use is Gen 2:4; Strong's number designation is H3068. Other words with same number is JEHOVAH, (Ex 6:3); and God, (Gen 6:5). What is the translation and possible usages?

Read Gen 18:13; 28:12; Ps 114:7; 118:28; 1Peter 1:25

13. As you've no doubt noticed, the word *God* or Lord doesn't always translate the same way. What are some differences in these interpretations?

14. The word *Lord*, not all caps, appears in both Old and New Testament, (KJV). Can you determine the difference in the following usages?
a). Hebrew (OT) translation of Lord, (H136), Gen 18:3; 18:27; 20:4?

b). Translation of lord, (H113), Gen 18:12; 19:18.

c). Translation of lord, (H1376), Gen 27:37.

d). Greek (NT) translation of Lord, (G2962), Matthew 1:20; 10:24; 1Peter 1:25; 3:6; Revelation (Rev) 1:8; 11:8.

e). Is there a difference in *God the Lord*, and the *LORD God*?

(Following puzzle for review and enjoyment).

Father of The Tribes—Early Years, Genesis 25:26–27:45

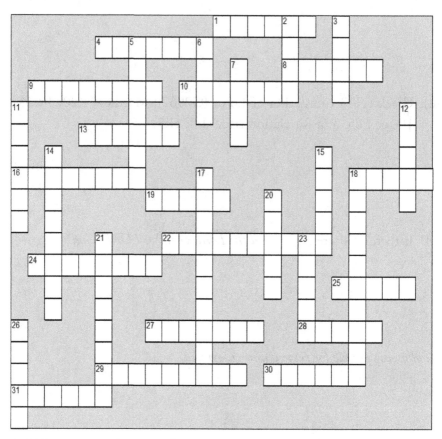

*All Scripture references from Genesis, unless otherwise indicated.

Across:

1. A few days with Jacob's uncle grew to be _____ years, (*Gen 31:41).

4. Israel's mother, (25:21-26; 27:11).

8. God changed Jacob's name to _____, (32:28).

9. Scripture says that Esau _____ his birthright, (25:34). (To 16A)

10. Esau often cooked savory _____ for his father's meal, (27:7; 25:28).

13. Jacob feared if he tricked his father, he would be _____, (27:12).

16. (From 9A) ...because he _____ it away without regard to the circumstances. (Hint: akin to traded).

18. Esau predicted to live by the _____, (27:40).
19. To escape Esau's wrath, Jacob went to his uncle _____, (27:43).
22. Israel was one hundred _____ years at his death, (2 wds), (47:28).
24. Jacob's brother and other relatives would be his _____, (27:37).
25. The sons of Israel are sons of _____.
27. Jacob obeyed his mother and _____ his father, (27:5-17).
28. Jacob was a plain man and dwelt in _____, (25:27).
29. Creator of puzzle content.
30. Jacob's _____ helped him deceive his father, (27:5-29).
31. There were _____ tribes of Israel, (49:28).

Down:
2. Esau was Jacob's _____ brother, (25:24-26).
3. _____ sold his birthright to his brother, (25:33; Heb 12:16).
5. Isaac _____ Jacob as first-born, rather than Esau, the older, (Gen 27:27-30).
6. At birth, Jacob held onto his brother's _____, (25:26).
7. Esau swore to _____ Jacob when their father died, (27:41).
11. The _____ of Israel are the sons of Jacob, (49:28, 33).
12. The skin of Esau was _____ and rough, (25:25; 27:11, 23).
14. Isaac's blessing of Jacob, instead of Esau, fulfilled the _____ of Gen 25:23.
15. To disdain, spurn, or despise.
17. The tribes were also called _____, (Acts 7:8).
18. The Hebrew translation for Jacob is _____, (27:36).
20. The clothes that Jacob wore smelled of the _____, (27:27).
21. Both Jacob's parents had a _____ son, (25:28).
23. The man, Israel, died in _____, (47:28-30).
26. Jacob's father was _____ years old when he was born, (25:26).

(Puzzle Answers found at End of Book, after Reference Tables)

~ 2 ~

~ Prelude ~
To The Kingdom

Background Scriptures:
Genesis 29:21-35; 30:1-24; 35:16-20
Lesson Scriptures: Various

"All these are the twelve tribes of Israel: and this is it that their father spake unto them, and blessed them; every one according to his blessing...." (Gen 49:28, KJV).

Jacob, the son of Isaac and Rebekah; Isaac, the son of Abraham and Sarah. Jacob was the father of twelve sons, had two wives, and two concubines. Jacob's wives, Leah and Rachel, were sisters. Leah was well aware of the fact that she was not Jacob's choice; she was the oldest daughter. Her father tricked Jacob into marrying her as the conditional agreement for him to marry Rachel. So, Leah had a husband. Now she would no longer be a burden to her father, but she was, and would remain, second to her younger sister.

The house of Jacob did not live happily ever after—there was trouble in the camp. God blessed Leah with children first, softening her status of secondary wife. She named her son Reuben, announcing, '*behold a son*', (Gen 29:31-35). She was boastful and proud of her accomplishment. God had seen her troubled heart and consoled her.

Leah's second son was Simeon, translated as *heard* or *hearing*. Leah was joyous because the LORD had seen her dilemma and given her another son. Then, twice more she gave birth to sons, Levi and Judah. Her consolation for Levi was thoughts of having Jacob more *attached* to her. In Judah, she gladly proclaimed Jehovah's *praises*. She had given Jacob four sons, while her sister had not birthed one child.

The sisters each had a personal handmaiden. Aside from tending their mistresses' daily needs, and caring for their children, they became surrogate mothers as well and concubines to Jacob. They had to listen to the children they brought into the world call someone else mother, as the sons they gave birth to could not be claimed as their own, Gen 30:3.[1][2][3]

Rachel wanted children desperately, and gave Jacob permission to bed her handmaiden, Bilhah. She hoped to acquire a son for her husband through Bilhah, and avoid the stigma of being barren. As previously mentioned, children born by such a union would be regarded as those of the wife, not the handmaiden.[4]

A woman with no children was seen as a curse directly from God, and could render a family extinct.[5] Bilhah came through for Rachel, giving birth to two sons; first Dan, then Naphtali. Dan, so named because Rachel felt God not only heard her cries, but also *judged* her. Naphtali, named thus because of Rachel's constant battles to outwit and out maneuver her sister, (Gen 30:8).

Not to be outdone, Leah gave Jacob her handmaiden Zilpah, to bare more children for her. Zilpah gave birth to two sons, Gad and Asher. Leah considered Gad as bringing her good *fortune*. In Asher, she felt truly blessed and *happy*. She, Leah, had six sons to her credit; Rachel only two, and those were not sons from her womb.

Having a maidservant bare children for you was an age-old custom from the code of laws instituted in Babylon years before by King Hammurabi.[6] Leah, Rachel, their maids, Rebekah, her brother Laban, Abram, Sarah, her hand-maiden—had all lived either in Padan-aram, or Ur of Chaldees, which is in Mesopotamia, and part of Babylonia. These families would be well aware of this code and its consequences.[7]

The daily competitiveness of the lives of Jacob's family was further demonstrated when Rachel and Leah negotiated for mandrakes. Besides their known mystic powers, and pleasant scent, described by Solomon,[8] this fruit had a very special effect—it intensified one's desire toward another. The Hebrew translation of this fruit is love-apple.[9] Rachel won the passion fruit, but Leah won Jacob for the night.

In due time, Leah gave birth to another son, Issachar. She reasoned God had *rewarded* her for having won Jacob's presence in her tent. She conceived again, giving birth to Zebulun. After six sons, Leah considered herself extremely blessed in having an outstanding dowry to entice and keep her husband with her. Of the four women to bare Jacob's children, Leah gave birth to the most—seven in all; one a daughter, Dinah. Leah was exuberant, and *exalted.*

The sons of Bilhah did not appease Rachel's desire to bear sons of her own. Childbearing is a major accomplishment looked upon favorably. A man could divorce his wife if she did not produce an heir.[10] In His appointed time, God opened Rachel's womb and she gave birth to Joseph, saying, *the LORD shall add to me another son,* (Gen 30:24).

Rachel did give birth to a second son and died after naming him Benoni, (Gen 35:18). Jacob renamed this son Benjamin, signifying that he favored a name implying a positive circumstance, rather than *son of my sorrow,* for which Benoni translates. Benjamin means *son of my right hand.* Genesis 44:18-20 describes Jacob's youngest son as *son of his old age.*

This book introduces the sons of Jacob, the twelve tribes of Israel. Jacob means *supplanter, heel holder,* or *deceitful.* Israel means *God prevails.* And so, Israel did, and they do, and they will. They are God's chosen peoples; the heart of God's promises to Abraham and his seed, which would grow to outnumber the stars. (See Gen 15:5; 22:17; 26:4; Exodus (Ex) 32:13; and Deuteronomy (Deu) 1:10; 10:22).

Read Genesis 29-30

1. Envy and jealousy was introduced early in Genesis by the behavior of Cain. The serpent also displayed covetousness, envy, and cunning behavior. Explain the difference between jealousy, envy, and covetousness.

2. How could Jacob possibly say to Laban, *'give me my wife'* rather than, *'give me my betrothed.'*

3. Laban explained his trickery in substituting Leah as bride to Jacob instead of Rachel. Describe Laban's suggested remedy for Jacob's dilemma.

4. A wedding in those days was more than just a ceremony. Research the meaning of *fulfill her week* in Gen 29:27; and Judges 14:12, 17.

5. In a matter of weeks, Jacob had two wives. Imagine if you were one of these women, sister or no, what kind of thoughts would be occupying your mind?

6a. We can't ignore how Jacob might have felt, or managed with two sister wives, and later two concubines. Envision the struggle of what he might have endured.

6b. Marrying sisters would later be against God's law, (Lev 18:18). Discuss.

7. Jacob's grandfather, one of the forefathers of the Jewish nation, slept with his wife's handmaiden and acquired a son of that union. (Gen 16). a). Who was this grandfather?

b). Discuss the son of the grandmother's handmaiden.

8. The sons born to Jacob by his wives' handmaiden were counted as part of his family, and received a blessing when Jacob died. Discuss why the son of Abraham's concubine wasn't given the same consideration as the sons of Jacob's concubines. (See Gen 21:9-21; Gen 49).

9. Jacob did not hide the fact that he loved Rachel, probably from the first time he saw her, (Gen 29:10-11; 18, 31-35). How did God intervene in favor of Rachel's sister?

10. Describe what these names reveal about Jacob's four women. Include Hebrew meaning.
a). Rachel

b). Leah

c). Bilhah

10d). Zilpah

11. Notice the tribes included in the 144,000 sealed servants spelled out in Rev 7:4-8. Your thoughts.

12. Discuss what you've learned from this study that helps you better understand Jacob, his wives, and his twelve sons.

(Word Search puzzle following for review and enjoyment).

Blessings for Twelve Sons
Genesis 49

Clues:

Father of Isaac

Yield up the ghost

God Almighty

God's gifts are a

Asher produced rich

Promised Land

Simeon, Levi displayed

Future judge

Naphtali compared to a

Reuben ____ father's wife

Seed

Yield up the ghost

Benjamin: a _____

Old eyes are

Pack animal

Joseph's mother

Also Bethlehem

Multiply; be ____

Our creator

More than

Enmity

Spiritual Jacob

Was to be slave

Son of God

_____ wolf, (2 wds.)

Jacob wrestled an ___

Judah a ____ cub

Joseph's firstborn

Gad literal means

Rod, staff, tribe

Dan said to be a ___

Jacob yrs. in Egypt

Scepter belongs to

Zebulun likened to

Gen 48:22 portion?

Puzzle content by

Rachel's sister

Answers:

Abraham	Descendant	Israel	Shiloh
Angel	Die	Issachar	Ships
A ravenous	Dim	Jesus	Shoulder
Blessing	Donkey	Leah	Tjjohnson
Bread	El Shaddai	Lion	Troop
Canaan	Ephrath	Manasseh	Wolf
Cruelty	Fruitful	Rachel	
Dan	God	Scepter	
Deer	Greater	Serpent	
Defiled	Hate	Seventeen	

Puzzle grid next page:

20

Blessings For Twelve Sons, Genesis 49

*Words found across, down, and in three diagonals in puzzle grid.

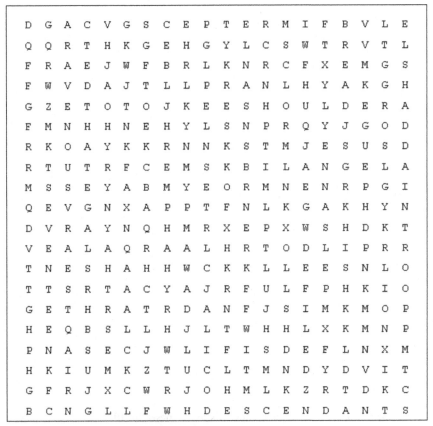

```
D G A C V G S C E P T E R M I F B V L E
Q Q R T H K G E H G Y L C S W T R V T L
F R A E J W F B R L K N R C F X E M G S
F W V D A J T L L P R A N L H Y A K G H
G Z E T O T O J K E E S H O U L D E R A
F M N H H N E H Y L S N P R Q Y J G O D
R K O A Y K K R N N K S T M J E S U S D
R T U T R F C E M S K B I L A N G E L A
M S S E Y A B M Y E O R M N E N R P G I
Q E V G N X A P P T F N L K G A K H Y N
D V R A Y N Q H M R X E P X W S H D K T
V E A L A Q R A A L H R T O D L I P R R
T N E S H A H H W C K K L L E E S N L O
T T S R T A C Y A J R F U L F P H K I O
G E T H R A T R D A N F J S I M K M O P
H E Q B S L L H J L T W H H L X K M N P
P N A S E C J W L I F I S D E F L N X M
H K I U M K Z T U C L T M N D Y D V I T
G F R J X C W R J O H M L K Z R T D K C
B C N G L L F W H D E S C E N D A N T S
```

(Puzzle answers found after Reference Tables)

~ Notes ~

[1] *Firefighter Cassette Tape Series.* Chuck Missler. Genesis 30, 1994
[2] Hammurabi Code, from *www.avalon.law.yale.edu*
[3] *The King James Study Bible.* Thomas Nelson Inc. 1988, Genesis 11:31
[4] *The New Unger's Bible Dictionary.* Moody, Revised and Updated edition, 1988, p146
[5] ibid footnote #4
[6] ibid footnote #2
[7] ibid footnote #3, #4
[8] ibid, footnote #3, Song of Solomon, 7:13
[9] *www.blueletterbible.org*
[10] ABC's Of The Bible. Reader's Digest Assn., Inc., 1991, ps146-147

~ 3 ~

REUBEN, PART I

Lesson Scriptures
Genesis 29:32; 35:22; 37:18-28; Various Deuteronomy

"And Leah conceived, and bare a son, and she called his name Reuben: for she said, Surely the LORD hath looked upon my affliction; ..." (Gen 29:32, KJV).

The first born! Presumptive heir of the firstborn's inheritance of his father's blessings, and riches. The eldest; the one his father would be bragging about. The one his younger siblings would look up to. The one who erased any anxiety of childlessness from his mother's heart. The first born! A son!

His name was Reuben, pronounced with a short (ü) as in shoe; and long (à) as in pay; as (ru-bane'). Reuben's name means *behold, a son; or see, a son.*[1]

Leah was overjoyed because she had conceived first. She was satisfied that God recognized her status as wife by default. He had given her a son; before Rachel. Jacob described Reuben as, 'my firstborn, my might, and the beginning of my strength, the excellency of dignity, and the excellency of power,' (Gen 49:3).

The Scriptures don't tell us exactly how much older Reuben was than his three brothers—Simeon, Levi, and Judah—born in succession after him. We do read where Reuben was a leader in some respects. He kept his siblings from harming their younger brother Joseph, as the story is told in Genesis thirty-seven. Jacob's boys conspired to kill Joseph because he was their father's darling. Besides that, Joseph talked about his dreams, which presented them in a subservient role to himself.

Reuben heard the plot against Joseph, and quieted the murderous thoughts of the others, (Gen 37:18-22). Reuben then devised a ploy to put Joseph in a pit, temporarily, to avert any killing. But, Reuben didn't hang around to see his plan through. In his absence, Joseph was sold to a group of traveling Midianite merchants, also known as Ishmaelites, (Gen 37:28).

When Reuben returned to retrieve Joseph, he found the place empty; Joseph was gone. Reuben knew instantly that he was in trouble. Their father's favorite son was missing! He panicked, wondering what he would tell their father. The schemers subsequently concocted another story involving tales of a ravenous beast devouring Joseph and leaving his bloody tunic behind.

Years later after Rachel died, Jacob traveled to a place described as *beyond the tower of Edar*, in Palestine.[2] As the elder son, Reuben had the honor of family leader while his father was away. Reuben considered this duty very lightly, or he took his role too seriously. Either way, he decided to test the limits of his authority as temporary family-head and claimed liberties with Bilhah, one of his father's concubines, (Gen 35:21-22).

The story tells us that Jacob heard of it; nothing more, nothing less. Just four words—'and Israel heard it'—relates Jacob's knowledge thereof. No circumstantial evidence, no contributing factors. When your father doesn't mention a serious error you've made, nor dole out punishment for it, or give you a guidance lecture to help you make better choices in future—watch out. It puts you on notice. You will never know when, or where, or how hard the hammer is going to fall. But you can be sure of it, the hammer will fall.

Delayed punishment, on the other hand, gives a person time to admit a mistake, show remorse for wrong-doing, and ask forgiveness. There is no indication that Reuben took advantage of that option. Perhaps he was afraid to face his father. He had displayed disrespect, disregard, selfishness, and sneakiness. In those days, a concubine was considered a secondary or inferior wife.[3] Also, it was considered a criminal offense if a concubine was unfaithful.[4] In the book of Judges 19:1-4, he who has a concubine is called her husband; the woman's father is father-in-law to her husband.[5] In Gen 37:2, a concubine is described as a wife.[6]

In this scenario, Jacob revealed some of our heavenly father's attributes. He showed mercy, patience, understanding, time for confession, time for forgiveness, and the ability to delay actions for future review. Reuben could have asked his father's forgiveness at any time—just as we all are invited to do when we are wrong.

Reuben's sin caught up with him when it was time for Jacob to bless his sons. Reuben's blessings did not include the double portion reserved for the first-born son, (Gen 49:1-4; 1 Chronicles 5:1; Deu 21:15-17). Reuben would not excel. He would never do as well as his brothers. Not superior; not outstanding; no over-abundance; no distinguished future. Just enough.

Read Gen. 49:1-4; 29:31-32; 32:22; 37:2; 35:22; Deu 21:15-17; 33

1a. The birthright of a firstborn son is a treasured inheritance. Research and discuss.

1b. Define the difference between a birthright and a blessing.

2a. In Mosaic law, there are guidelines pertaining to children of a wife who is loved, and a wife not loved. Research and discuss whether this applied to Jacob. Why or why not?

2b. Discuss the difference between a wife and a concubine of that era.

2c. Did Jacob consider Bilhah and Zilpah as concubines, or as wives?

3a. Could the son of a concubine inherit as a firstborn? Research, give references. (See also Gen 16-18:18).

3b. What rights did a concubine's son have? See Keturah and Abraham. (Gen 16:10-12; 17:20; 21:13; 25:1-9).

Read Genesis 49:1-4; 37:1-33
4. How are the following phrases interpreted?
a). Excellency of dignity

b). Excellency of power

5a. Review the jealousy and hatred of Jacob's sons towards their brother Joseph. What fueled their hatred?

5b. In the plan to kill Joseph, Reuben was the deciding vote that kept him alive. What do you think motivated Reuben's actions?

Read Genesis 35:16-22; Deu 22:22 &30; 27:11-20
6. After Rachel died, Jacob traveled to a place called *Tower of Edar*. What is the translation of this place, and where is it located?

7. While Jacob was away, Reuben betrayed his father by sleeping with one of his father's concubines. What could have prompted such behavior?

8a. The law that God gave Moses came after the Israelites were delivered from Egypt. Research what might have been the punishment for Reuben's actions.

8b. Discuss the implication of Reuben's choice of concubine.

9. Reuben, along with five of his brothers, has a strange assignment in Deuteronomy 27:13. Discuss the implication of this charge by Moses.

Read Genesis 49:1-4; 1Chr 5:1
10a. When and how was Reuben's punishment discussed by his father?

10b. Name the blessing Reuben received.

10c. Did Reuben's portion represent a blessing or a curse?

11a. What son actually received the firstborn portion? Discuss these implications.

11b. Discuss the relationship between Joseph and Reuben.

~ Notes ~

[1] *www.blueletterbible.org*
[2] ibid footnote #1, Genesis 35:21
[3] *The New Unger's Bible Dictionary.* Moody, Revised and Updated edition, 1988, p251
[4] ibid footnote #3
[5] *The King James Study Bible.* Thomas Nelson Inc. 1988, Judges 19
[6] ibid footnote #5

~ 4 ~

Reuben, Part II

Lesson Background: Genesis 42; Exodus 2-4; Numbers 1, 2 & 25
Lesson Scriptures: Various

'...Behold, I have heard that there is corn in Egypt: get you down thither, and buy for us...; that we may live, and not die.' (Gen 42:2, KJV).

At a time when there was a shortage of food in Canaan, Reuben and nine of his brothers went to Egypt to buy corn, for corn, or grain was plentiful there. (Gen 42:1-5). In Egypt they found someone they didn't think they would ever see again.

Years before, when Joseph's brothers sold him to traveling merchants, they had no idea where he would end up. But here he was. In Egypt. In charge. A governor! They would have to deal with him for anything they hoped to buy. They would have to bow down to him—the one they had hated, the dreamer.

Joseph recognized them right away, and he accused them of spying. He demanded they go back to Canaan and return with their youngest brother Benjamin. Once there, Reuben tried negotiating his two sons as ransom, to convince his father to allow Benjamin to go with them back to Egypt, (Gen 42:37). Reason one, to prove they had a younger brother back home; two, to prove they were not spies; three, to obtain

Simeon's release; four, to keep their word to the governor of Egypt; and five, to buy the food they sorely needed.

During the time when Israel wandered in the desert, they carried their tabernacle with them wherever they traveled. The LORD traveled with them and dwelled among them in the wilderness, (Exodus 25:8.) When the tribes were on the move, the tabernacle—also called the tabernacle of the tent of the congregation, or sanctuary, moved too, (Num 2). This holy place of worship was constructed in such a manner as to be easily set up or taken down as the LORD directed.

When the tribes were immobile, Moses stationed each tribal camp in a predetermined position surrounding the tabernacle, (Num 2:1-2). Reuben's location was south of where the tabernacle stood. The tribes, or families, of Simeon, and Gad shared the south camp along with Reuben. The entire armies of Reuben, Simeon, and Gad were 151,450 men strong, (Num 2:10-16). Reuben's tribe numbered 46,500 men. The men counted had to be twenty years or older, and able to go to war.

Some of Reuben's descendants were among those who were swallowed up—killed, along with all their families and everything they owned—because of their plan to undermine the authority of Moses and Aaron. These men had accused Moses and Aaron of trying to be more holy than all the other men of the congregation. Dathan and Abiram of Reuben's tribe, with Korah of Levi, and another two hundred forty-seven men, defied God by refusing to follow the leadership of Moses and Aaron. They reasoned that all the tribes of Israel were holy unto the LORD, and entitled them to have identical authority as Moses and Aaron, (Num 16; Ex 29; Deu 11:1-12).

God did not like this. The priesthood was a special service and privilege given only to Moses, Aaron, and the sons of Aaron. Therefore, the perpetrators were in defiance of God's Holy Word to Moses, who delivered God's commands to His people. So, the people separated themselves from those guilty of trying to usurp God's elect, and God punished the guilty.

The earth then opened her mouth and engulfed houses and men; wives and children; everything that was theirs vanished into the ground. In addition to the big sinkhole, the LORD sent a fire to consume those who unlawfully offered incense in His Holy Tabernacle, (Num 16:31-35). The children of Korah were not destroyed because Korah had sanctified the tabernacle, (Num 26:5-11).

Another plague wiped out twenty-four thousand people because of their worship of false gods and alliances with forbidden peoples. After that, the number of Reuben's men dwindled to 43,730 men, (Num. 25-26:10).

Upon reaching the borders of the land God had promised, the tribes began to think about where they'd like to settle. Men of Reuben and Gad liked the land of Jazer and the land of Gilead, because it was very favorable for raising cattle, (Num 32:1). Gilead was on the east side of the Jordan River, and described as—this side of Jordan—for it was situated before the Israelites crossed over into the land of Canaan, (Num 32:29-42).

It was agreed that Gad, Reuben, and one-half of the tribe of Manasseh would take possession of this land. It had been the kingdom of Sihon, king of the Amorites; and the kingdom of Og, king of Bashan. The Reubenites, the Gadites, and one-half tribe of Manasseh also claimed all the cities of the countryside nearby. This would be their home.

Read Genesis 46:9; 1 Chronicles 5:3

1.   Reuben fathered four sons. Name and note their name translations.

Read Genesis 42

2a. There was a famine in Canaan. Your thoughts on why it took ten men from Canaan to go to Egypt for food. Who were they?

2b. Who did these men do business with in Egypt, and what was his title?

3a. Discuss the situation in Egypt that afforded that city to have food when other cities didn't.

3b. Joseph was taken to Egypt as a young lad. Review extenuating circumstances.

4a. Give a synopsis of Joseph's initial interview concerning his brothers' identities.

4b. Simeon was taken hostage and jailed while his brothers returned home. Why Simeon?

4c. Explain the implication of Joseph's request to have Benjamin come to Egypt.

Read Numbers 1-2:17; 2 Samuel 24; Deuteronomy 33:6
5. God told Moses to count the men of each tribe who were 20 years old and up. What initiated this action?

6a. During David's kingship, the numbering of Israel displeased God. Why was the numbering that Moses did different?

6b. Compare the number of men in Reuben's family with those of the other tribes. Discuss how Deuteronomy 33:6 impacts Reuben's sons.

7a. Events noted in this chapter indicate a need to count Israel again. Why was that count necessary?

7b. Is there a disparity in this count and the previous count for Reuben's tribe? What brought about this change, and what was the result?

7c. Reuben's camp was assigned a specific position in relation to the tabernacle. Discuss location and the tribes that accompanied Reuben.

Read Exodus 33:7-17; Ex 40:34-38
8a. What was the importance of the Tabernacle of the Congregation?

8b. Describe the Hebrew translation of *tabernacle* and *congregation*.

Read 1 Chr. 6:2-3; Num. 16:1-35; 26:1-11, 59; Ex. 2:1-10; Ex. 3-4, 6:18-20

9a. Of which tribe were Moses and Aaron?

9b. Both Moses and Aaron had different responsibilities to the tribes. What were they?

10a. Men of Reuben's family were guilty of trying to overthrow the authority of Moses and Aaron. Discuss the situation.

10b. What was so terrible about these rebels' actions that God judged them severely?

10c. Of the 250 men condemned, who from Reuben's family were involved?

10d. One family of those guilty was spared this punishment. Discuss why God was merciful to them and not the others.

Read Numbers 32:1-5; & verses 29-42

11a. Reuben and two other tribes claimed their inheritance before they crossed west over the Jordan. Which land did they claim, and why was that land so appealing?

11b. Who were the other tribes who desired land in proximity to Reuben?

11c. There were issues that had to be settled before the question of their land grant could be decided. Discuss.

12a. Can you find a New Testament descendant of Reuben?

12b. Retrace the outlay of Reuben's territory on any map and name a modern-day city located there.

~ 5 ~

SIMEON

Background: Genesis 34; 37; 42; 43; & 46;
Numbers 1; 2; & 10
Lesson Study: Various

"Simeon and Levi are brethren; instruments of cruelty are in their habitations. Cursed be their anger...and their wrath...: I will divide them in Jacob, and scatter them in Israel." (Gen 49:5, 7 KJV).

Simeon was the second son born to Jacob and Leah. Simeon's name was decided by his mother's perception of her circumstances and her fate. She knew the LORD was aware of her situation, and she thanked God that He had given her another son. His name is pronounced as (shim on') with a long (ô); sounding like (shim'own). The name translation infers *hearing* with acceptance, hearkening, and understanding.[1] God had heard and compensated her case.

Not much is said of Simeon early in scripture. He earned a ruthless reputation for being heartless and cruel when the families lived in Shalem, a city of Shechem. They had journeyed there after meeting, and seemingly making peace, with Jacob's brother Esau.

When Esau and Jacob last parted company, their agreement was to meet in Seir, the country of Esau or Edom, (Gen 33:1-20). However, as

Esau and his men returned to Seir, Jacob took an extended detour to the north by way of Shechem, to a town called Succoth.

Shechem is also where the family lived during the time Joseph went missing (Gen 37:12). Bible history relates Joseph as feeding the flock along with his brothers. Joseph's brothers, named in the early verses of Genesis thirty-seven, were the sons of Bilhah and Zilpah. All of Joseph's brothers hated him, except maybe Benjamin. It is not clear if he had been born yet, and if he had, he may have been too young for herding the flock, (Gen 35:16-20; 37:1-10;). These men detested Joseph, and never had a kind word to say about him. The reason was simple: their father loved Joseph more.

Furthermore, Joseph dreamed grand dreams, and told his family about them. As a result, his brothers hated him even more, leading to the plot to kill him. The story mentions that Reuben and Judah were somewhere near the flock; along with the sons of Bilhah and Zilpah, (Gen 37:21-30).

No doubt, Shechem was a memorable and tragic place for Jacob's family. This was not only the place where the family lived when 'a ravenous beast' supposedly attacked Joseph, but also where Dinah was assaulted. One day she had ventured away from the family to explore the sights of the city. Perhaps being the only girl among so many boisterous, bossy, and protective brothers, she longed for the friendship of other young women. During her excursion, she was apprehended and seduced by Shechem, a man who lived in the area. He was the son of Hamor, who was a family boss himself, and prince of that country, (Gen 34:2).

Shechem asked his father to get Dinah for his wife, meaning please consult with her father to win Dinah as his wife. But; however; a most serious transgression had been committed—Shechem had defiled Dinah! And Jacob heard about it! And, so had her brothers! It didn't matter if the young man loved Dinah, and spoke kindly about her, and to her, and wanted to marry her. He had defiled her! This terrible action against Dinah is defined as rape in today's culture.[2]

After all the negotiation for Dinah's hand in marriage—the men of Shechem consented to be circumcised, and the date and time set. However, brothers Simeon and Levi never intended to honor any word they gave about these arrangements. Instead, they released their revenge on the town. Scriptures say they slew the men and took Dinah out of the house of Shechem. They also plundered the city, taking houses, wives and children, sheep, oxen, all their wealth: everything Hamor owned.

To add to their sister's ordeal, Simeon and Levi added misery to ruination. Jacob was appalled by the outlandish behavior of his sons. He described himself and their family as being the stink of the land, (Gen 34:30). In addition to that, he worried about retaliation against his family, who was smaller in number than the surrounding nations. So, Jacob re-located his family to Bethel.

During the famine in Canaan, Simeon was among the search party that traveled to Egypt to buy food. The governor of the land, the brother they had sold as a slave years earlier, accused them of being spies. He asked, rather he demanded, that they return home and come back with their younger brother, whom they said was left behind. This would not go well with their father, though it was the only way they would be able to buy food from the landlord of Egypt.

Looking back, to that time of long ago, these same boys had delivered Joseph to traveling Ishmaelites—enemies of theirs. They didn't know if Joseph was still alive or not, or how he had fared. They had liberated themselves of their father's favored son, which had been their immediate concern at the time.

Unknowingly, they were now living at the mercy of that brother, their father's beloved. And as Jacob had accepted that Joseph was dead, he held close to Benjamin, the son of his right-hand.

At any time when the tribes camped, or traveled with the tabernacle of the congregation, each tribe had a specific place in the camp, and a specific order in which they assembled. Simeon's family was assigned alongside the family of Reuben, due south of the tabernacle. Simeon and Gad's families marched with Reuben whenever the colossal site was disassembled to go forth to another location, (Num 10:17-36). The total of Simeon's men—20 years old and up, fit to go to war—were 59,300 (Num 2:10-13).

As the families approached their 'Promised Land' they camped at Shiloh. Joshua, now their commander, sent three men from each tribe to survey the land and bring back pertinent details about their future home. While they waited for the representatives to return, they were sure to be thinking about what their portion would be. Although some designations had been decided before, they had not yet crossed the Jordan to possess it. Joshua cast lots to allocate equitably between the tribes yet to receive shares of Canaan land west of the Jordan, (Joshua 18:10).

Simeon inheritance fell within the land allotted to Judah. This included the cities mentioned in Joshua 19:1-9; some cities have same or similar names, (Josh 15:20-63).

Notice that the tribes to inherit were not the original twelve. Two and one half tribes settled on the east side of the Jordan River; nine and a half tribes settled on the west side of the Jordan. Simeon's family was counted with the nine and a half tribes. Also, the tribe of Levi was not eligible to receive a land grant. They had a special dispensation, as discussed in the Levi chapters.

Read Genesis 29:33-35

1. Look-up Hebrew translation of Simeon's name.

2. Simeon was full brother to who?

Read Genesis 33:18—34:31

3a. Discuss the brother who was in league with Simeon in seeking revenge upon the men of Shechem.

3b. After her ordeal, how would you describe Dinah's mood, or her feelings about the man who wanted to marry her? Did she have any say in the whole matter?

4a. Discuss the outcome of the agreement Jacob made concerning circumcision of Shechem's men.

4b. Why was Dinah in Shechem's house? Look also at rules of betrothal. (Ex 21:8-11, 22:16).

5. Jacob was enraged by Levi and Simeon's behavior. Discuss the tongue lashing they received.

6. Jacob decided to move, again. Where did they run to this time?

Read Numbers 2:10-13, 34

7a. God prepared Israel to defend against opposition as they traveled through enemy territories. How many men of war in Simeon's family?

7b. Discuss Simeon's assigned post when they were camping in the wilderness. What was the importance of assigning specific positions?

Read Exodus 6:15; Numbers 26:12-14; 1 Chronicles 4:24-27
8. Name the sons of Simeon and the translations of their names, Gen 46;10).

Read Numbers 34:16-20; Joshua 19:1-8
9a. After conquering the inhabitants living in the land of Canaan, the parceling of ownership ensued. Describe land granted to Simeon.

9b. Did Israel drive out the people of the land they inherited? What was the outcome of their attempts? Give references.

Read Deuteronomy 33
10. Moses blessed the tribes before he died. How did Moses bless Simeon?

11. Find a New Testament relative of Simeon. Research spelling and translation of Simeon.[3, 4, 5] (Acts 13:1; Luke 2:25; Luke 3:30).

12. Describe the outlay of Simeon's territory, and name a modern day city of that location.

---

[1] www.blueletterbible.org
[2] *Reader's Digest, ABC's Of The Bible.* Reader's Digest, Inc., 1991, p99
[3] *Smith's Bible Dictionary.* Thomas Nelson, 1986, pg632
[4] www.blueletterbible.org
[5] The King James Study Bible. Nashville: Thomas Nelson, 1988.

~ 6 ~

LEVI, Part I

Background: Genesis 29:31-34; 34:25 & 30
Exodus; 1:1-6:30; 28-32
Lesson Study: Various

"And she [Leah] conceived again, and bare a son; and said, 'Now this time will my husband be joined unto me, because I have born him three sons:' therefore was his name called Levi." (Gen 29:34, KJV).

Another son born to Leah and Jacob. Leah had no problem fulfilling her duties as a wife: she was producing sons to carry forth the seed and name of Jacob. Leah, three sons; Rachel, none. Leah thought that surely now Jacob would be more attentive and devoted to her; be *attached* more readily to her, (Gen 29:34). She was first wife, and she longed for first rights. She wanted Jacob to be her husband, more so than Rachel's.

Looking at the translation of Levi's name, we discover the meaning is to be *joined* or *attached*. Levi is derived from (lâváh), meaning to adhere. This gives insight to how Leah might have decided to name this son.[1] The pronunciation of Levi is: (lâ vê); long (a); long (e); sounding like (lay vee), with emphasis on (vee).[2] He is full brother to Reuben and Simeon, born before him; Judah, Issachar and Zebulun after him.

Levi is next mentioned in reference to the vengeance heaped upon the man who took liberties with his sister, Dinah. Only he and Simeon attacked all the men of the town, not just Shechem, who was guilty of the assault of Dinah. Negotiations commenced when Shechem requested to marry Dinah. Levi and Simeon were not having it, even though they led Hamor, father of Shechem, to believe all would be forgiven if every man of the town would consent to be circumcised. Not just Shechem, all the men!

What a serious price to pay for a wife! However, Dinah's marriage was not the only one to be negotiated. The agreement would allow all men of Shechem to marry the daughters of Israel, (Gen 34:9, 16). And the men of Israel would marry the daughters of Shechem. Big woof! These guys were not even joking. They never meant a word they spoke to Hamor and Shechem.

Centuries later, Moses was called upon to carry out the promise God had given his people. The promise Jacob had heard from his father; and Isaac from his father Abraham; and Abraham from God himself. God promised Israel a property as far as the eye could see. God affirmed and reaffirmed this promise to Abraham, to Isaac, and to Jacob, (Gen 50:24).

At his appointed time, Moses followed through with the charge given him to lead Israel, (Ex 3; 33:1). This journey took him through forty years of barren wilderness; mumbling, grumbling, stubborn people; hunger and thirst; fear and trembling; hostile people; wars, and threat of wars; believing God, not believing God; obeying God, not obeying God; having God as their protector day and night; and having God angry with them because of their short attention span. But God loved Israel, and intended to keep His promise, though many who left Egypt didn't make it to their dream land, including Moses and Aaron.

God directed Moses through every step of the journey. Moses spent many days in God's presence, gathering knowledge and directives to carry back to God's people. One command was to count the number of men worthy for defending Israel against attack from other nations. The total readiness of those men, twenty years and older, came to six hundred three thousand, five hundred fifty, (603,550) men. This number exceeded half a million men—women and children were not counted, (Ex 38:26; Num 1).

The tribe of Levi was not included in the census for fighting battles; they were exempted from fighting. God had an equally important, but more solemn and spiritual mission for them—they were to be dedicated to the service of the LORD. The LORD is their inheritance, (Deu 10:8-9; 14:27-29; 18:1). The tribe of Levi also did not receive land as their brothers did, but they were awarded cities from each brother's portion, spread across the face of the Canaan countryside.

Levi fathered three sons: Gershon, Kohath, and Merari. Aaron, the first priest unto God, was a descendant of Levi, (Ex 6:16-20). Aaron fathered four sons: Nadab, Abihu, Eleazar, and Ithamar, (Num 3:2-4; 26:57-61). Two of Aaron's sons, Nadab and Abihu, died when they offered strange, unsanctioned fire unto the LORD. Any sons, grandsons, great-grandsons, and descendant sons of Aaron were to serve in the office of priest to the LORD, (Num 3:5-10). Aaron's successor was his eldest surviving son, Eleazar.

Read Genesis 29:31-34
1. Discuss the translation of Levi's name.

2. Leah was especially pleased when Levi was born. What did she hope to gain with his birth?

Read Genesis 34

3a. Jacob's only daughter suffered an unfortunate and disgraceful ordeal. Do you think Levi and Simeon were alone in planning such a murderous retribution against the perpetrator, and the entire town?

3b. One aspect of the marriage agreement involved the men of Shechem marrying the daughters of Israel. Which daughters would these be?

3c. Would those marriages have pleased Rebekah? Why or why not? References.

Read: Genesis 45 through 47:27-31

4a. Recount how Jacob's family got to Egypt from Canaan.

4b. Discuss Jacob's departure from Egypt.

5. God gave Abram a vision concerning Israel's bondage in Egypt. Name the specifics of that vision, (Gen 15; Ex 12:40-42).

Read Exodus 3; 4:10-17; 6:16-30; 12; Numbers 26:59
6a. Name the charge God gave Moses to lead Israel out of Egypt.

6b. What are your thoughts on God's choice of Moses for this assignment?

6c. Where was Moses when God gave him directives concerning Israel?

7a. Aaron was charged to assist Moses. Why? When? Where?

7b. Name the parents of Moses and Aaron, and their tribal ancestors.

8a. Israel was enslaved in Egypt for a very long time. The original twelve sons had long since died. Discuss the number of years they were captive in Egypt, and conditions in which they lived.

8b. Under what circumstances did the nation of Israel leave Egypt? Condense please.

Read Exodus 32

9. During a time when Moses communed with the LORD, Aaron made a golden calf for the people to worship. God didn't punish Aaron for this despicable action. Why do you think God was so merciful to Aaron?

10. Identify the mountain where Moses spent time with God. It is known by multiple names; give two.

11. Research and discuss a New Testament descendant of Levi.

12. What have you learned about the tribe of Levi and Israel from this lesson.

~ Notes ~

[1] *Smith's Bible Dictionary.* Thomas Nelson, 1986, p357

[2] *www.blueletterbible.org*

~ 7 ~

LEVI, Part II

Background: Genesis 29:31-35; 49;
Exodus 13:2-16; Numbers 2; 3
Lesson Study: Various

"And the LORD spake unto Moses, saying, Bring the tribe of Levi near, and present them before Aaron the priest, that they may minister unto him. And they shall keep his charge, and the charge of the whole congregation before the tabernacle of the congregation, to do the service of the tabernacle." (Num. 3:5-7, KJV).

This lesson concentrates on the special dispensation of the Levi tribe. In particular, how and when they received their assignment as priests to the nation of Israel, and what they were expected to accomplish.

The Bible indicates the presence of priests long before Moses anointed those of the Levitical order. Before the time of Moses, the position of priesthood was held by the head of the family, the father; or by the head of a tribe.[1] Joseph married Asenath, the daughter of Potipherah, the priest of On, (Gen 41:45). Jethro, the father-in-law of Moses, was priest of his family, and of Midian, the area where Moses ended up after fleeing Egypt, (Ex 3:1; 18:1). Job also sanctified his family, and offered burnt offerings as a sin offering for his sons, (Job 1:5).[2]

Melchizedek—interpreted as king of righteousness, was also king of Salem—interpreted as king of peace, and is mentioned as a priest of the most-high God. Melchizedek blessed Abram, offered him bread and wine, and described Abram as being 'of the most-high God, of heaven and earth.' Abram, in response, gave tithes of all he had to Melchizedek, (Gen 14:18-20; Heb 7:1-10).

Other men built altars and offered burnt offerings to honor and give thanks to God. The first altar in Scripture was built by Noah, (Gen 8:20). He had weathered the great flood with his family in a wooden ark full of animals of every kind. Abram/Abraham, Isaac, and Jacob also built altars, offered sacrifices, and purified and consecrated themselves, and their families, (Gen 12:7-8; 13:18; 22:1-14; 26:25; 33:18-20; 35:1-3).[3]

The sacrifice Abraham prepared to offer God in Gen 22:9 was Isaac, his own son. Abraham's faith was being tested. When God was satisfied that Abraham truly trusted him, He interceded on Isaac's behalf. God showed Abraham a ram, provided especially for this sacred occasion; the ram was to be sacrificed instead of Isaac. The miraculous appearance of a specific animal, caught in a nearby bush, high on a mountain top, declared Abraham's answer to Isaac, (See Gen 22:8). Specifically, and prophetically that God would provide himself a lamb!

In this chapter, we again witness God showing His authority and direction. He preempts the practice of priests as heads of families. But, before God institutes the special office of priests, he called Israel out of bondage. As stated previously, God directed Moses to go back to Egypt, to his old adoptive family, and take his people, Israel, from their hard living, and slave-masters they had endured for centuries.

Moses was hesitant, made excuses for himself, particularly his manner of speech. God discounted that impediment, and named Aaron as Moses' spokesman. Together they went to Egypt, to Pharaoh. And the 'let my people go' series of tests proceeded. God won. Israel left Egypt with God leading them and the Egyptian army chasing them. They had nowhere to go except into the Red Sea. The Hebrew expression for *Red Sea* is *sea of reeds*; originating from reeds, weeds, or rush water plant, (Ex 10:19; Jonah 2:5).[4, 5] The people of Israel made it through; Egypt's army did not.

Out of Egypt; away from slavery, on their own; anxious about where they were going; Pharaoh's army chasing them; and other hostilities awaiting them. How would they manage food, water, heat, cold, sleep, families; even being led by Moses, whom they didn't entirely trust? These are things Israel was sure to have thought about as they emerged from the Red Sea and began their long journey.

In the wilderness of Sinai, Moses got further direction from God. He revealed that Israel would be a kingdom of priests, a holy nation to Him, (Ex 19:6). After another commune with God, Moses brought back the stone tablets which God had written, (Ex 24:12-18). It was during this time when God told Moses that Aaron, and Aarons' sons, would be special envoys to Him as priests. They were destined to be consecrated to Him, and represent the holiness of His people, (Ex 28-31).

The Levite tribe would be responsible for the care of the Tabernacle of the Congregation; to take it down in readiness to move forward, and set it up again when their movement ceased. They were accountable also for transporting the tabernacle, and caring for the various vessels used in their worship to the LORD, (Num 1:47-54).

Why was the Levite tribe chosen to receive special privileges? Why were they selected as God's special envoys? Why was Moses chose to lead them? These answers belong to God, (Deu 29:29). It is interesting to note that when Moses came back down the mountain after his first forty-day conference with the LORD, Aaron, one chosen to be set apart, had led God's people to sin. At the urging of the people, Aaron created a golden calf as a god, and built an altar for burning offerings, (Ex 32). But when Moses asked who was 'on the LORD's side', the tribe of Levi stood with Moses and with the LORD, (Ex 32:25-29).

The entire tribe of Levi were inducted as ministers unto Aaron, and his sons after him. God chose the Levites as the first-born sons He wanted to be set apart unto Him for selective service. This was a reminder to Israel of their freedom from Egypt. The first-born sons of the Egyptians had died, but the first-born sons of Israel were spared. (Ex 12:12-16; 34:19-20; Num 3).

God lead Israel for many days protecting them with cloud coverage from the sun by day, and a fiery pillar at night that provided light and heat. After construction of their portable tabernacle, He gave guidance on how Israel was to travel, or pitch their tents, having the tabernacle in their midst. The tabernacle was surrounded by the Levites, and the Levites were surrounded by the camps of their brother tribes. This was by God's own design to protect the tabernacle, and the congregation of Israel, (Num 1:50-53).

Neither Moses nor Aaron were allowed to enter into Canaan land. After bringing the children of Israel to the precipice of God's promises, these two titan leaders were prevented from proceeding further. They had neglected to follow God's specific directions, and give God the glory He required in the presence of His people. Numbers chapter twenty tells the story of how God was disappointed in his servants' disobedience. Unlike Aaron, Moses did get a birds-eye view of that beautiful land, Israel's future home, (Deu 34:1-12).

Lesson Discussion:
Read Numbers 3:4, 6:16-7; Exodus 28:1; Leviticus 10:1, 26:60-61
1. The LORD gave detailed instructions for His tabernacle.
a). Who anointed and sanctified the tabernacle? How was this done?

b). Explain the difference in anointing and sanctifying.

c). Why was the ark of the covenant so important?

d). Who were the first custodians of the ark of the covenant?

2. Before the temporary tabernacle was built, how had God communicated with his people? Give references.

Review Ex 28; Num 1:47-51; 3:1-13; 8:5-26; 18; Lev 8

3a. The tribe of Levi was chosen to be a special exemption for the LORD. When was this assignment made known to them?

3b. Why do you think God chose the Levites for special assignment?

4. God doesn't tell us all there is to know about him. Name the scriptures which explain what is written for our benefit, and that which is not. Give advantages, and disadvantages.

5a. From which son of Levi were the priests' descendants of? Name the priests at that time.

5b. Not all Levi descendants were priests. What were duties of men who were not priests?

6a. The high priest performed an exclusive service when he came before the LORD in the most holy place. Name the high priest and discuss his specific role. (Ex 28:30-43).

6b. Describe the garments of the high priest. Briefly mention details of these garments, including the precious stones.

6c. Research the circumstance of Exodus 28:34-35 when the high priest could be in danger of death. (See also Num 18:1-3; 25-32).

7. The first man called priest of the most-high God lived long before Moses or the Levites. Who was this priest, and what impact did he have? (See also Hebrews 7:1-10).

8. Discuss the role of Moses and his association with the priests and the tabernacle.

9. Identify and describe the following and their importance:

a). Tabernacle

b). Sanctuary

c). The Ark

10. Two of Aaron's sons committed an unforgivable sin. Research and discuss what happened with Nadab and Abihu, (Lev 10:1-2; Num 3:4; 26:61).

Review Num 1:53; 2; 3:14-51; Ex 25

11a. When the tribes of Israel were not on the move, they had a pre-determined formation in setting up their campsite. Discuss the significance of the positions of Aaron's sons during these times.

11b. Expound on the special circumstances associated with the Levites, and their dedication to the service of the Lord.

11c. Whose responsibility was it to transport the ark and other artifacts belonging to the tabernacle? (Num 3:27-32).

Review Ex 19:6; Num 18:1-32; Num 8:6-20; Num 35:1-8

12. The Levite tribe did not receive a portion of the land promised their fathers. Name the Levites inheritance pertaining to:

a). The LORD's service

b). Tithes from fellow tribes

c). Dwelling places in the new land

13. Discuss the gifts God required each tribe to bring to the tabernacle, and their important to the recipients.

Review Ex 13:1-16; 34:19-20; Num 3:38-51; 8:13-19; 18:20-21

14a. What was God's priority for the firstborn of Israel? Name his reasons for this requirement.

14b. How many of Israel's firstborn were dedicated to the LORD?

~ Notes ~

[1] *The New Unger's Bible Dictionary.* Moody, 1988, p1029
[2] ibid
[3] ibid
[4] www.blueletterbible.org
[5] ibid #1, p1069

~ 8 ~

JUDAH, Part I

Lesson Background: Genesis 37; 42-45
Lesson Scripture: Genesis 29:35; 38 & 49:8-12

"And she conceived again, and bare a son: and she said, Now will I praise the LORD: therefore, she called his name Judah; and left bearing." (Gen 29:35, KJV).

A fourth son for Leah! What happiness! She declared, 'Now will I praise the LORD.' She called him Judah, pronounced as (yeh-hoo-daw) or (yeh·hü·dä'), and translated as *praised, celebrated;*[1] *praise Jehovah* or *confessions of Jah.*[2] These words mean the same thing, just stated differently by individual authors. By this stage in your studies, you've probably noticed that Jacob's wives named the children. The only son he named was Benjamin, Rachel's second son, (Gen 35:16-18).

Scripture doesn't report much about Judah in his early years. He was part of the plot to punish Joseph because of his dreams, and, his good fortune in being their father's choice. Judah may not have been involved in the decision to kill Joseph, but he was surely part of the conspiracy. They had agreed to the story invented to tell their father, so they had to stick together. And they were successful in that deception, for Joseph's tragic imaginary event rang true in Jacob's ears. Good fortune, or conscious torture? Time always reveals the end result.

In Genesis 37:25-27, it was Judah's idea to profit from the disappearance of Joseph. Judah even calculated the price they should receive; Reuben insisted there be no bloodshed. One wonders where the rest of the tribe was during these discussions. They all envied and hated Joseph. Could Simeon, Levi, Issachar, and Zebulun have been tending another herd at a different location? Where was Dan, Naphtali, Gad and Asher?

Shortly thereafter, the Bible reports that Judah left his father's home and traveled to Adullam, where he met and married a Canaanite woman. He and his wife had three sons: Er, Onan, and Shelah. The two older men did not do well, as the LORD killed Er and Onan. Er was wicked, and Onan had the misfortune of displeasing God. Much later, Judah fathered twins, Pharez and Zarah, by the former wife of his sons. Her name was Tamar. Genesis chapter thirty-eight documents Judah and Tamar's story.

When Judah and his brothers went searching for food during the great famine, he took the lead in relating demands of the governor of Egypt to their father. Judah convinced Jacob to permit Benjamin to accompany them back to Egypt, as specifically requested. For the governor, had assured them nothing would be decided until Benjamin came back to Egypt with his brothers.

Once Benjamin was in Egypt, Joseph wanted to detain him as a hostage. Judah conveyed concern that Jacob, their father, would surely die if Benjamin didn't return home with them. Plus, this would not go well for Judah; he would certainly fall out of favor with his father. After extensive negotiations and tests, Joseph finally divulged his true identity. They wept, hugged, kissed, expressed remorse for past deeds, made amends, and finally forgave one another.

The interpretation of Judah's name suggests that he would be blessed. According to the words of his father's blessings in Gen 49:8-12, Judah's brothers would praise him. When praises go up, blessings are returned. Jacob blessed Judah, naming him as chief ruler over his brothers. He is described as a lion cub, then as an old lion. His young sons portray noble qualities, especially the son bound to the choice, or noble vine, which yields purple grapes and produces the richest and finest wine.[3] This wine analogy is further described as the blood of grapes, (Gen 49:11).

The sceptre spoken of in Gen 49:10 indicates a mark of authority, as in kingship, lordship, even messiahship. It also depicts a rod, staff, branch offshoot, or tribe. The seed of Judah would produce lawgivers—kings— who would rule until the time of Shiloh, signifying the Messiah.[4]

The Messiah is from the 'root of Jesse,' the father of David, descendant of Judah, (Is 11:10; Rom 15:12; Rev 22:16). In Apostle John's revelation, He is riding a white horse; His clothing splattered with blood— suggesting the sacrifice which poured from His body when He died to pardon our sins, (Rev 19:11-16).

That most precious blood of Jesus fulfilled the death penalty which was levied on all sinners. His death paid the required penalty of our sins, meaning that we sinners are cleansed by the blood He spilled as He died, forgiving us all. However, to be covered by, and included in that merciful act, we must belief in *who* He is, and accept *why* He died. We must sincerely seek His forgiveness for our sins by simply asking Him to forgive us. In time, other things will become clear: His earthly death; His resurrection and return to Heaven; and His eventual return for those who believe in Him. All who believe will be gathered together with Him where He is, and remain with Him forever! (Rom 10:9-11; 1Thes 4:13-18; 1Cor 15:51-57).

Read Genesis 29:35; Exodus 6:3; Psalm 83:18

1. One of the translations of Judah's name is *praise Jehovah.*

a). Research which Hebrew word Jehovah is derived from.

b). How do *you* praise Jehovah?

Read Genesis 37, 38

2a. Discuss where the family lived when Judah left home and married.

2b. Explore the custom of marrying a deceased brother's widow to provide the dead brother an heir.

3. Who was Tamar in this passage?

4a. Why do you suppose Onan objected to fathering a child with Tamar?

4b. Discuss your thoughts of God's displeasure with Onan.

5a. Judah promised his youngest son, Shelah, as a husband to Tamar. What happened?

5b. One would think that Tamar would have had enough of Judah men after Shelah reneged and didn't marry her. Discuss her revenge plan.

6. Judah mistook Tamar as a harlot. Was his judgment fair? What were his before and after attitudes?

7a. Instead of gaining a grandson from Tamar, Judah gained two more sons. Translate the meaning of their names.

7b. Judah's twin boys are reminiscent of another set of twins. Compare Gen 38:27-30 with Gen 25:21-26.

Review Genesis 42; 49:1-12

8a. Joseph accused his brothers of spying when they came looking for food. Why?

8b. Reuben blamed his brothers for the dilemma they were in. Later Judah took over negotiations. What were their tactics?

9. Approaching the end of his life, Jacob blessed his sons. How was Judah's blessing more prominent than his brothers?

10. Discuss Judah in relation to each phrase below.

a). A lion cub

b). An old lion

c). Young sons

d). Noble quantities

e). Finest wine

f). Sceptre or Scepter

g). Shiloh

h). Root of Jesse

i). Messiah

j). Blood of grapes

~ Notes ~

[1] Smith William, L.L.D., *Smith's Bible Dictionary*, (Thomas Nelson, 1986), pgs. 326-327.

[2] Unity, *Metaphysical Bible Dictionary*. (Unity School of Christianity, 1931), p372.

[3] *www.blueletterbible.org*; (Tools; Interlinear; choice vine; H8321)

[4] Ibid; (Tools; Interlinear; Shiloh; H7886)

~ 9 ~

JUDAH, Part II

Lesson Background: Genesis 38; 42-45; Numbers 1; 3; 4; Numbers 10; 13; 26; Deuteronomy 33; 2 Kings 24; 25
Lesson Scripture: Various

"Judah, thou art he whom thy brethren shall praise: thy hand shall be in the neck of thine enemies; thy father's children shall bow down before thee." (Gen 49:8, KJV).

Judah Praised. Celebrate Jehovah.[1] He was designated such honors since birth. An incredible expectation to live up to. There is not much proof of deeds to be praised in the formative years of Judah's life; nor in the development of his young adult years. Evidence of his becoming a leader is shown later by his willingness to act as negotiator for food in Egypt, (Gen 43:8; 44:14-34).

In the wilderness of Sinai, the tribe of Judah numbered 74,600 men, (Num 1:26-27). In assigning camping and protective positions, Judah's men were assigned first, due east of the tabernacle. Two tribes appointed with Judah were Issachar and Zebulun. These three tribes of 186,400 men had key positions, (Num 2:1-9).

Several of the chapters in this book relate how the remaining nine tribes had similar designations for camping and marching with the tabernacle.

Most scriptures describe the tabernacle of the congregation as the place of God's presence, (Ex 27:21). However, the following listing depicts more descriptive purposes:

- tabernacle of testimony, (Ex 38:21)
- tabernacle of witness, (Num 17:7)
- tabernacle of the LORD, (Lev 17:4)
- tent of the congregation, (Ex 40:22)
- Sanctuary, (Ex 15:17; 25:8)

This temporary, movable structure housed the dwelling place of God; the place where the LORD communicated with his servants during their journey across the desert lands.

Moses anointed and sanctified the tabernacle, after which the heads of each tribe were required to bring an offering before the LORD. The house of Judah was first to bring gifts. Their contributions were extensive, (Num 7:10-17). Issachar and Zebulun's gifts were bestowed on separate days following Judah's presentations. Other tribes gifted in a similar pattern.

Whenever Judah was required to move, so did the two brother tribes assigned with him, as standard procedure. The camp of Judah led first, upon the sounding of an alarm. They also took lead position when alerted to assemble at the door of the tabernacle to hear Moses; or when the camp settlement was disassembled and moved from one location to another, as they traveled toward their homeland. Each group followed accordingly, as the LORD commanded Moses to assign them.

Along with a lead tribe, and order of position, each unit had a significant banner. In any situation involving the tribes—whether they were camping, marching, or defending themselves—they were identified by their ensign, i.e., a flag, banner, or emblem, (Num 2:2-9). Though individual tribes had an identifying banner, each camp was recognized by the banner or flag of the captain. For example, Judah, as captain of the Eastern boundary, was known by an emblem of a lion, as was his camp, (Gen 49:9, Rev 5:5).

For each identifier, there is a correlated insight in scripture. Judah is shown as an image of a lion; Reuben as a man; Ephraim as an ox, or calf; and Dan as an eagle. In some scripture, depending on which Bible translation you use, cherubs or cherubim(s) are said to be of a celestial nature—a figure of a man, an ox, a lion, and an eagle, (Eze 1:10; 10:9-14; Rev 4:6-8; 5:5). On the Blueletterbible.org website, eagles are related to a serpent; an eagle changes its feathers; a serpent sheds its skin.[2, 3 4]

As stated in other chapters, God ordered Moses to number the men of Israel several times. The first time was in the wilderness of Sinai, after the tabernacle of testimony was completed, (Num 1). The second count determined the number of Levites who would be dedicated unto the LORD, redeeming all the first-born of Israel, (Num 3). Thirdly, Numbers chapter four outlines the assignment of the work of the tabernacle to the able-bodied Levite men aged thirty to fifty. Fourth count took a census of the tribes to equitably divide the inheritance of their new homeland, (Num 26).

As Moses was not allowed to advance into the land of promise, he blessed each leader before going up the mountain of Nebo, where he viewed their precious, promised land before he died. Moses used few words in blessing Judah when compared to those given by his father. Notice the difference in the following blessings:

From Moses:
Deuteronomy 33:7
"And this *is the blessing* of Judah: and he said, Hear, LORD, the voice of Judah, and bring him unto his people: let his hands be sufficient for him; and be thou an help *to him* from his enemies."

From Jacob:
Genesis 49:8-12
"Judah, thou *art he* whom thy brethren shall praise: thy hand *shall be* in the neck of thine enemies; thy father's children shall bow down before thee.

"Judah *is* a lion's whelp: from the prey, my son, thou art gone up: he stooped down, he couched as a lion, and as an old lion; who shall rouse him up?

"The scepter [sceptre] shall not depart from Judah, nor a lawgiver from between his feet, until Shiloh come; and unto him *shall* the gathering of the people *be*.

"Binding his foal unto the vine, and his ass's colt unto the choice vine; he washed his garments in wine, and his clothes in the blood of grapes:

"His eyes *shall be* red with wine, and his teeth white with milk."

From Historical Records:
1 Chronicles 5:2
"For Judah prevailed above his brethren, and of him came the chief ruler;"

Judah's tribe was destined for greatness. His offspring would eventually produce influential and famous kings. Beginning with King David, there was a king of Judah. That is, until King Nebuchadnezzar of Babylon took Judah's people captive. However, in attacks during the period from 606 to 586 B.C., the plunderers left the poorest of the people behind, (2 Kings (Ki) 25:8-12).[5]

There were also kings of Israel, so named when the twelve tribes split, (See 2 Sam 2:8-10, 17; 1 Ki 12:1-17; 2 Ki 15:29-17:23). Ten tribes formed the Tribes of Israel, known as the Northern tribes; two tribes formed the Tribes of Judah, or the Southern tribes. In 734 to 721 B.C., Israel was first taken captive by Assyria.[6] Babylon defeated Assyria in 605 B.C. and took both Israel and Judah captive.[7, 8]

Even so, the prophecy of a King of kings, a Lord of lords, the Messiah, was not to be denied, (Gen 49:10; Isa 9:6-7; Rev 17:12-14; 19:6, 16).

After a time in servitude, Jehoiachin, the surviving king of Judah, was released from prison in Babylon and given special privileges, (2 Ki 25:27-30; Jer 52:31-34). So, the Judean kings' legacy continued even unto the times of the New Covenant—the New Testament.

Scriptures and stories are written and rehearsed in songs of the baby king snuggled in an animal feeder in Bethlehem. A brilliant star led wise men and shepherds on that holy, silent night. The prophesied King, the long-expected King of Judah, the King of all kings had been born! They called his name Jesus! He *was* the Christ! The Anointed! His mission: to liberate humanity from the slavery of sin. He *is* the Chief Ruler! He *is* the Messiah! Our Liberator! Our Savior! He *is* the King! He *is* the LORD! Our Lord! Our Majesty!

Review Genesis 43:1-34; 46:26-29

1. Express your thoughts on Judah's success in bringing Benjamin to Egypt when Reuben's appeal failed.

Read Numbers 2, Genesis 3:23; 4:16; 12:8; 25:6

2. The word *east* carries a certain connotation in Jewish culture. Research and discuss.

3. Judah defended the east side of Israel's camp when they were immobile, and led the camp whenever they traveled. Express importance.

4. Explore the bonding relationship between Judah and the tribes of his camp.

5a. Give a scripture reference for the banner of Judah.

5b. How important were banners/flags in Israel's time? In our time?

Read Genesis 49:8-12; Deuteronomy 33:7
6a. Can you decipher the blessing Moses imparted to Judah?

6b. Which of Jacob's blessings impresses you most? Why?

6c. How did Judah prevail above his brothers?

Read 1 Samuel 16:13-23
7. Why do you think God chose a man, not of Judah, as first king of Israel? Who was he, and of which tribe was his forefather?

8. The first king from the line of Judah was much loved and influential. Who was he? Research and discuss a couple of his accomplishments.

9. The term 'Jew' is derived from the name 'Judah'. Research how, and why? Give scripture references.

10. Find a New Testament descendant of Judah's tribe, other than Jesus. Discuss.

~ Notes ~

[1] Unity; Metaphysical Bible Dictionary. Unity School of Christianity, 1931, p372.

[2] Missler, Chuck; *The Camp of Israel*. (Koinonia House Ministries, 1993).

[3] Brindle, Wayne A, et al, eds. *The King James Study Bible*. (Nashville: Thomas Nelson, 1988).

[4] www.blueletterbible.org

[5] Halley, Henry. H; *Halley's Bible Handbook*. (Grand Rapids. Regency Reference Library, Zondervan, 1965), p210-211.

[6] ibid, p212

[7] ibid, p212

[8] ibid, Brindle, pg653 (Notes, v23:28, 29).

~ 10 ~

DAN, Part I

Lesson Background: Genesis 30; 42-49;
Lesson Scriptures: Various

"...Behold my maid Bilhah, go in unto her; and she shall bear upon my knees, that I may also have children by her. ...And Rachel said, God hath judged me, and hath also heard my voice, and hath given me a son: therefore, she called his name Dan." (Gen 30:3; 6, KJV).

Rachel had much to contend with, given the circumstances in marrying the man she loved, and then being denied motherhood. She was so frustrated that she demanded a miracle of her husband. When Jacob reminded her of his limitations in the matter, she decided to try a different approach— she resorted to the centuries-old custom of condoning the union of your hand-maiden and your husband. In this manner, your maid might give birth to a son for you. So, Rachel gave Bilhah to Jacob to produce a son in her stead. A child born from such a union between your maidservant and your husband would be considered your child, not the servant's.[1, 2]

No doubt, this was not an easy decision for Rachel to make. She could envision how the other women would *judge* her; what they would say. She, unable to have children; her maiden, sleeping with her husband. She could become the laughingstock of the whole camp! Years before, Sarah, Jacob's grandmother, had done the same thing in giving her handmaiden to her husband Abraham, to produce an heir. In the case of Jacob and the maids of his wives, neither the children nor their mothers became outcasts. They remained members of the family.

Dan was born to Jacob, and Rachel, and Bilhah. His name is pronounced as (Dān; short a), and can be interpreted several ways: *judge*, ruler of righteous *judgement*, defender, or advocate.³ He was the first son of Jacob to be born to a servant. Did the other boys tease Dan about his birth mother? Scripture doesn't say, but human nature has not changed. Would the other half-brothers be mocked? Ishmael and Isaac had different mothers also, and Ishmael mocked Isaac; teasing, ridiculing, taunting—whatever worked for his purposes.

There is sketchy history of Dan. Jacob's blessings to this son seems to be conflicting. He was labeled a judge for his people in one verse; a serpent in the next, (Gen 49:16-17). Moses described Dan as a lion's whelp, a young lion or cub, (Deu 33:22). A lion's whelp is the same phrase that Jacob used in blessing Judah, (Gen 49:9).

Dan was honored when the LORD chose Aholiab, one of his family, to have wisdom of heart. Aholiab was equipped to work as an engraver, an embroiderer, a weaver, and a teacher. He worked along with Ori of Judah, in workmanship of the tabernacle of the congregation, (Ex 31:6; 35:31-35). Another son brought Dan dishonor when he cursed and blasphemed the name of the LORD, using God's Name in a blatantly contemptible and dishonorable manner. This man's father was an Egyptian; his mother an Israelite. The son is not named, but he was stoned to death for cursing God, (Lev 24:10-23).

Lesson Discussion: Various Scriptures

1a. Discuss Hebrew translations for Dan's name. Give References.

1b. Discuss the fact that the first mention of Dan comes before the record of his birth. (Gen 14:14).

2. Research how Egyptian culture crept into Israel's way of life.

3. Who were Dan's closest family allies?

4. Childhood teasing can influence one's personality and development. Imagine Dan's formative years.

5. Explore how teasing might have affected the relationship between Isaac and Ishmael.

6. In what way does the translation of judge fit Dan's character?

7. Describe Dan as:
a). A Lion cub

b). A serpent

8. We may all have relatives, or acquaintances, we'd like to keep at a safe distance. Do you know someone with Dan's characteristics?

9a. How would you describe the term, 'from Dan to Beersheba'? List your references.

9b. Where is the city or territory of Dan? Where is Beersheba? What are surrounding territories?

10. Find and expound on a well-known New Testament descendant of Dan.

~ Notes ~

[1] Brindle, Wayne A, et al, eds. *The King James Study Bible.* (Nashville: Thomas Nelson, 1988).
[2] Hammurabi Code, from _www.avalon.law.yale.edu_
[3] Unity, Metaphysical Bible Dictionary, 1931, p164.

~ 11 ~

DAN, Part II

Lesson Background: Genesis 30; 42-49
Lesson Scriptures: Various

"Dan shall judge his people, as one of the tribes of Israel. Dan shall be a serpent by the way, an adder in the path, that biteth the horse heels, so that his rider shall fall back-ward." (Gen 49:16-17, KJV).

A first impression of Dan might be the sparse details about his tribe's history. In Moses' assessment of the tribes' land inheritance, only one son of Dan is mentioned—Shuham, (Num 26:42-43). Only one son, Hushim, is mentioned in Gen 46:23. Of threescore and two thousand, seven hundred men, only two were named in a positive manner.

It is noted in *The New Unger's Bible Dictionary* that the name Hushim is written in plural form, indicating a family, not a singular name. The wilderness count of Dan's tribe revealed 62,700 men aged twenty and up; (Num 1:38-39). Only God and the writer of the Torah know the mystery of singular listings in the Biblical genealogies of Dan.

Dan's tribe was the last to inherit land as specified in Joshua. Their limited allotment incensed the family leaders who claimed they were cheated. The land was not nearly enough to satisfy them, so Dan's tribe went to war against Leshem, forcefully taking the city located near

Mount Hermon. Leshem, also called Laish, was later renamed Dan after their tribal father, (Joshua (Jos) 19:47; Judges (Jud) 18).[1]

The tribe of Dan even set up a graven image and named their own priests, which was forbidden, (Judges 17:7-13). Jonathan, the son of Gershom, who was the son of Manasseh, and the sons of Jonathan, were priests to the tribe of Dan until the day of their captivity, (Jud 18:27-31; Deu 29:1-28). This was indicative of a time when people did what they considered right, according to their own thoughts. No kings. No judges. No priests.

During the time of the Southern and the Northern Kingdoms, King Jeroboam had two golden calves made for the people to worship—one placed in Bethel, the other in Dan. This is reminiscent of the Sinai revolt. The Israelite king (re: Northern Kingdom), also chose priests from the lowest of the people; not from the sons of Aaron, (1 Ki 11:26-41; 12:25-33; Ex 28:1).[2] The book of Amos even refers to a 'god of Dan' in chapter eight, verse fourteen. God punished the offenders, as He does not ignore those who ignore His commands.

Various listings of the twelve tribes omit the tribe of Dan, though there are always twelve tribes in any given recording. This is apparent when either the Levites are included, or not. Then again, Dan may not be listed if the two adopted sons of Jacob are named in the tribal accounting, (Gen 48:5-6).

Revelation chapter seven designates 144,000 men as sealed servants of God. These are named as the twelve tribes of Israel; twelve thousand representatives from each tribe. Dan's tribe is not mentioned. Revelation chapter twenty-one, verse twelve says the twelve tribes are written on the twelve gates of the New Jerusalem, however, there are no names to associate with each gate.

When camp designations determined where each tribe would align them-selves surrounding the tabernacle, Dan's tribe was last to be assigned. He was leader of his camp, situated north of the tabernacle and accompanied by the tribes of Asher and Naphtali. Their combined total was 157,600 men; Dan's tribe accounted for 62,700 of that number, (Num 2:25-31). In reference to being the last tribe to be assigned, they were also last in procession whenever Israel traveled. This assignment carried with it the essential responsibility of rear guard, in times of battle and in ensuring safety, (Num 10:25-28).

Dan's tribal flag is designated as that of an eagle, according to Koinonia House Ministries.[3] Leviticus chapter eleven defines an eagle as being an abomination—repugnant and loathed; categorized along with several other birds, including vultures, (Lev 11:13). The eagle is a bird of prey, with keen eyesight, and known to be extremely fast. [4] They are also considered to be beautiful, majestic birds, especially when in flight.

Lesson Discussion: Various Scriptures
1a. If you are brave enough, discuss a time when you ignored God and did what you thought would suffice.

1b. Can you admit to the idols you give as much time, or more, than you do to the LORD?

1c. Discuss how money can be an idol, especially when we often give less in tithes and offerings than we do to things not of God.

2. What are your thoughts on the genealogy of Dan's tribal tree?

3. Describe Dan's land grant and why they might have felt slighted.

4. Israel did a good job in passing history on to their children. How could anyone have been so careless to ignore God's instructions about the duties and services designed for priests only?

5a. Explain who was qualified to serve as priests for the LORD.

5b. Who was qualified to serve as high priest?

6a. Define priests in present day vernacular.

6b. Are priests required or necessary for followers of Jesus? Give reasons and references.

7. What is the implication of a rear-guard assignment?

8a. Discuss the pros and cons of the eagle symbology.

8b. How does the eagle relate to Dan? Give references.

9. What is translation for the city 'Laish'? Where is it located?

10. Name a New Testament relative of Dan.

~ Notes ~

[1] www.blueletterbible.org
[2] Halley, Henry. H; *Halley's Bible Handbook.* (Grand Rapids. Regency Reference Library, Zondervan, 1965), p2s 193-196.
[3] Missler, Chuck; *The Camp of Israel.* (Koinonia House Ministries, 1993).
[4] en.Wikipedia.org

~ 12 ~

NAPHTALI, GAD, & ASHER

Lesson Background: Genesis 30; 42-49
Lesson Scriptures: Various

Naphtali:
"And Rachel said, With great wrestlings have I wrestled with my sister, and I have prevailed: and she called his name Naphtali." (Gen 30:8, KJV).

Rachel was so distraught at not being able to have children, she sent Bilhah to Jacob a second time. This must have been a hard decision for Rachel, as she competed with her sister, but perhaps not as much anguish as there was before Dan was born. This uneasiness and struggling also lends insight to the name Naphtali, pronounced as (naf-taw-lee'), and means *wrestling*. [1]

Naphtali's future associated him with a loosed hind, released or sent away. Oddly enough, the hind is a feminine noun, referring to a doe, mountain goat, or gazelle. The word even suggests a female association with the common stag. [2] An additional description pairs the hind with a great ram, indicating mildness or modesty. [3] Naphtali was said to speak elegant and kindly words, (Gen 49:21).

Moses spoke of Naphtali as full of blessings from the LORD, possessor of the south and the west, and satisfied with favor, (Deu 33:23). Naphtali was one of the tribes assigned to stand on Mount Ebal to pronounce curses upon those who did not live according to the commands of the LORD. Other tribes with this same tasking were Reuben, Gad, Asher, Zebulun, and Dan, (Deu 27:11-26).

Gad:

"And Zilpah, Leah's maid bare Jacob a son; And Leah said, A troop cometh: and she called his name Gad." (Gen 30:10-11).

Leah didn't bear children during the time Rachel's maiden Bilhah was pregnant with Dan and Naphtali. But later, not wanting Rachel to have an advantage, Leah offered Jacob her maiden Zilpah. When Zilpah gave birth to a son, Leah named him Gad, (pronounced as gäwd, with a star sound). In translation, Gad indicates a sense of distribution, signifying a multitude of fortune. Therefore, a fifth son to Leah's credit gave her a confident sense of good fortune—a *troop* of fortune. The Hebrew word for troop is gad.[4]

Jacob predicted that even though Gad would be overcome by a troop, he would emerge the winner. This is an interpretation that paints Gad as a division; a company of men; a band of soldiers, (Gen 49:19).[5] Evidence again that word translation is contingent upon subject matter.

Moses blessed not only Gad, but also those who would enlarge Gad. He was said to dwell as a lion, and slash both shoulders and heads; a fierce warrior, (Deu 33:20). As his inheritance, Gad chose rich, fertile land before the crossover into Canaan; including all the cities of Gilead, (Jos 13:24-28).

Asher:

"And Zilpah, Leah's maid bare Jacob a second son. And Leah said, Happy am I, for the daughters will call me blessed: and she called his name Asher." (Gen 30:12-13).

Asher, the second son of Zilpah, brought Leah great happiness. The name Asher is pronounced as (aw-share, as in the word awesome). His name is translated as *happy*, or *fortunate*. Six sons would surely gain Leah favor with her husband and bring compliments from the daughters of Israel. The LORD had blessed her again; she was indeed thankful and happy.

The blessings of Jacob directed Asher's hopes toward producing luscious bread, and royal dainties, (Gen 49:20). Before his death, Moses predicted that Asher would be blessed with children, be favorable to his brothers, and dip his foot in oil, (Deu 33:24-26). It is not clear whether previous Deuteronomy references speak of Asher's shoes alone, though his feet are destined to dip into oil. Still, in verse twenty-six, Jeshurun, meaning upright one, is a symbolic name for all Israel.[6]

Napthali, Gad, & Asher:

After their exit from Egypt, in keeping the LORD's commands, Moses determined the number of men aged twenty and older from each tribe. This survey, during their layover in the wilderness of Sinai, indicated the tribe of Naphtali to be 53,400 men. Gad's tribe was at 45,650 men. Asher's numbers were 41,500 men. These totals indicate men able to participate in war, as there would be numerous battles before they reached their land of promise, (Num 1 & 2, & numerous Old Testament references).

Gad's assigned position for camping and traveling was to the south of the tabernacle, along with Reuben and Simeon. Total number of Reuben, Simeon, and Gad in the wilderness was 151,450, (Num 2:16).

Asher and Naphtali shared a campsite position and rear marching orders with Dan. Their location was situated to the north of the tabernacle. The total number of men for Dan, Asher, and Naphtali, were 157,600 when they were in the wilderness of Sinai, (Num 2:25-31).

The totals of Israel's men showed strength in time of battle, and assisted in other tribal matters. During their forty-years of nomadic living, a great many families were killed in plagues, from other misfortunes, or died of natural causes. Knowing this, Joshua ordered another count in preparation for their procession across the Jordan River into Canaan. Also, before taking possession of the new land, an appropriate tally needed to be known to verify records, and properly divide and assign ownership. Their numbers totaled 601,730 in Moab, before the crossing. This did not include women and children; even the Levites were included in that calculation, (Num 26:51).

Receiving a land grant, and taking possession of the land is discussed in Joshua nineteen for each tribe. Gad's family representative decided to stake a claim before Israel crossed over the Jordan River into the west. Other tribes who had similar preferences were Reuben and a half tribe of Manasseh, (Num 32; Joshua (Jos) 13:24-28). Land allocated to Asher came in the fifth lot, as described in Joshua, (19:24-31). Naphtali's inheritance came in the sixth lot, (Jos 19:32-39). Part of Naphtali's land assignments included Kedesh, in Galilee, a city of refuge in Mount Naphtali, (Jos 20:7; Jos 21:32, and 1 Chronicles (Chr) 6:76).

Lesson Discussion: Various Scriptures

1a. What options did Bilhah and Zilpah have in following orders to sleep with the master of the house, (Gen 30)?

1b. Frustration and tension had to exist between four women who shared children with one man—in the same household. Can you name a few?

2. Is there any evidence that Naphtali, Asher and Gad, were involved in the disappearance of Joseph? Give references.

3. An evil report hints toward some irregularity in the activities of Jacob's sons tending the flocks. What could these reports have revealed? (Gen 37).

4a. Discuss Naphtali as a loosed hind.

4b. How does wrestling describe Naphtali?

5. Give an example of Gad as:
a). A troop of fortune

b). A troop of soldiers

6. Describe your thoughts on royal dainties of Asher.

7. In the wilderness, Asher and Naphtali merged with Dan's camp. Discuss the position of the tribe of Gad. (Num 2:25-31).

8. Moses and Jacob blessed each tribe, (Gen 49:16-21; Deu 33:20-24). Name blessings for these tribes.

a). Naphtali

b). Gad

c). Asher

d). Dan

9a. What was the importance of numbering the tribes as they journeyed from Egypt to the Jordan River? (Num 1 & 26).

9b. Explain the significance of crossing the Jordan River.

10. Cite a New Testament connection of:
a). Naphtali

b). Gad

c). Asher

11. Discuss a NT figure who had a ministry in the territory of Naphtali. (Gospels). Give references.

12. Review land allocation of the tribes, and their neighbors as shown in a map drawing. See following page, or use your choice of map.

Tribes Land Allocation According to Joshua in Moab

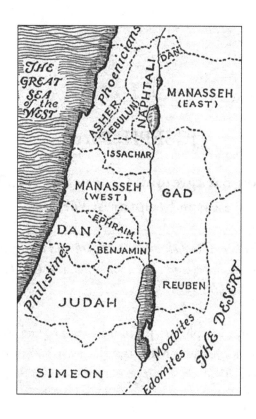

https://www.blueletterbible.org/images/TheGraphicBible/imageDisplay/tgb_032b[7]

[1] www.blueletterbible.org
[2] Smith, William, L.L.D., *Smith's Bible Dictionary*, Thomas Nelson, 1986, p249
[3] ibid, Smith
[4] ibid, #1
[5] ibid, #1
[6] ibid, #1; (Jos 14:1—19:51; Judges 18:1-31; Genesis 33:5)
[7] ibid, #1

~ 13 ~

JOSEPH, Part I

Lesson Background: Genesis 30; 37; 39-50
Lesson Scriptures: Various

"And God remembered Rachel, and God hearkened to her, and opened her womb. And she conceived, and bare a son; and said, God hath taken away my reproach:" (Gen 30:22-23, KJV).

Rachel called him Joseph; her precious, long-awaited son; the favored son of her husband. Joseph's name translates as: *adding*, or let him add. *The New Unger's Bible Dictionary* interpretation is: *may he*, [Jehovah] *add.*[1]

Joseph's name could be interpreted as Rachel speaking prophecy, referring to Benjamin, as in 'shall add another son', (Gen 30:24). Although the annotated translation, with Joseph the son added, can also refer to adding to the sons which Bilhah gave birth to. These were sons whom Rachel considered to be her own.[2, 3, 4] Pronunciation of Joseph taken from the Blue Letter Bible website is (yô safe').[5]

During the years that Jacob spent living on his father-in-law's land, Laban acquired eight grandsons; eleven, counting those of surrogate birth to his daughters. These children of Jacob, including daughter Dinah, were born in Syria of Padan-aram, or Mesopotamia, (Gen 28:2,

5, 7). After the birth of Joseph, Jacob bargained with Laban for blessings to take his family back to his home country, (Gen 30:25-43; 31:17-21).

Not much is said of Joseph's upbringing until the story of his spying on his brothers in chapter thirty-seven of Genesis. This passage states that Jacob loved Joseph more than his other children, and that Joseph, the first son of his beloved Rachel, was the son of Jacob's old age.

During that time, Joseph was seventeen and often joined his brothers in feeding the family flock. He was accustomed to picking up titbits of information about them to carry back to their father. These reports must have disclosed information that was of concern to Jacob; he sent Joseph for the specific purposes of discovery, (Gen 37:2-3; 12-14).

Older children rarely prefer having their younger siblings follow them around. This is true even when they love each other. But Joseph's brothers hated him, and definitely did not want him around. Their hate stemmed from the fact that Jacob made no attempt to conceal that he loved Joseph more. He gave Joseph a beautiful garment made with various colors, which can't be said for any of his other sons. Partiality given to one sibling creates a sour taste in the soul of the others. It also seems logical that the snitching Joseph did probably fanned the dislike they had for him.

And, if that wasn't enough reason for friction in the family, Joseph told them about his dreams. These dreams were graphic and momentous, prophetic even. One dream likened Joseph to a sheaf, rising high above other sheaves as they bowed low. The sun, the moon, and eleven stars paying obeisance to Joseph's sheaf was portrayed in another dream. This was enough to make them nervous, but not inquisitive. However, his father perceived some importance in what Joseph dreamed and thought seriously about it. (Gen 37:4-11).

So, bragging about his dreams, reporting his brothers' activities back to their father, and owning a beautiful piece of clothing, put Joseph at risk for ridicule and danger. One day their envy and hatred pushed them into murderous retaliation. They could not stand his presence, nor bragging, any longer.

Seeing Joseph coming from a long way off, possibly swaggering with self-confidence, prompted a plot to be rid of him, (Gen 37:18). First idea was to kill him and blame a wild beast, but Reuben dispelled that thought. He suggested putting Joseph in a pit somewhere in the wilderness rather than killing him. Evidently, Reuben left them and returned later to retrieve Joseph from the pit. But, Joseph was not there!

Joseph was sold to traveling merchants, and ended up in Egypt, first as a servant to one of Pharaoh's guards. Joseph progressed from servant to master of Potiphar's house; from house-master to imprisonment; from prisoner to prison guard; from prison guard to dream-teller of the Pharaoh; from interpreter of dreams to master of the land of Egypt. The LORD was with Joseph and made him prosper in all that he did. He excelled as the LORD blessed him and his work, (Gen 39:2-3).

Joseph's favor with Pharaoh began when he discovered Joseph's gift to interpret dreams. Pharaoh had dreamed two similar dreams, in detail, but no one could tell him what they meant. The butler remembered how Joseph had interpreted his dreams when they were in prison together. After two years, he finally had an opportunity to say something good to Pharaoh on Joseph's behalf, (Gen 41:1-14).

Pharaoh called Joseph out of prison to decipher his dreams, and praised him for having such talent. Joseph declined praise for doing anything of his own accord, giving all credit to God. Pharaoh was pleased to find out what was about to happen in his kingdom. He also recognized that *the Spirit of God* was in Joseph! He immediately promoted Joseph, giving him the signet ring from his finger, which gave Joseph the sign and seal of authority. Joseph was supplied with new linen clothing and a golden chain, which is defined more like a collar to be wrapped around his neck.[6] He was also appointed as second commander to Pharaoh in all of Egypt, (Gen 41:39-57).

Joseph had come a long way from beleaguered shepherd boy to beloved and trusted ruler over the realm of Egypt. It had been thirteen years since he was sold as a slave in Canaan, then sold again to an Egyptian captain of Pharaoh's guard. It would not be long before his boyhood dreams would materialize and progress as real historic and prophetic events.

Lesson Discussion: Various Scriptures

1. Joseph's name signified being added to the family. Determine the importance of his birth:

a). To Rachel

b). To Jacob

c). For Joseph

2a. Joseph's father had left Canaan to find a wife in Mesopotamia. Why was a woman of this land preferred over a woman of Canaan?

2b. Joseph's grandfather had also taken a wife from another land. Who was Joseph's grandfather? Great-grandfather? Which land was his grand-father's wife a native of?

2c. Explain why Joseph's great-grandfather was considered a stranger to Canaan. (Gen 11:27; 15:1-21; 17:8).

3. Where is Shechem located? Dothan? Give translation of these names.

4. Joseph often reported his brothers' behavior to their father. What could have been Jacob's concern? (Gen 37:12-14).

5. Nothing describes what Joseph might have felt about the merciless way his brothers treated him. What are your thoughts? (Gen 37:18-28; 42:21).

6a. Scriptures site a journey into Egypt as 'to go down'. Deliberate. (Gen 42:38; 43:4; 46:3).

6b. A return trip out of Egypt reads 'to go up'. Why? (Gen 44:33: 50:6).

7a. Expound on the background of the merchants who delivered Joseph from the pit where his brothers had left him, (Gen 37:27-28, 36; 39:1).

7b. Joseph was sold to an officer, a captain of Pharaoh's guard in Egypt. Research and discuss how *officer* is translated in this scenario.

8. God's blessings were with Joseph in whatever he did. Follow his resume from the captain's houseman to governor of Egypt, (Gen 39-41).

Read Genesis 41:14-32

9. God gave Joseph the meaning of Pharaoh's dreams. What was the interpretation of thin and withered ears devouring the well-fed ears?

10. Pharaoh had a similar dream, with cows instead of corn. What was significant about this dream?

Read Genesis 41:16, 39-45, 50-52; 48:1-22

11. God was delighted when Joseph rejected praise for interpretation of Pharaoh's dreams, (Gen 41:16). Explain.

12. Pharaoh was delighted; no more anxiety and disrupted sleep. He showered Joseph with gifts. Explore the significance of the following:

a). The name change, and meaning

b). A signet ring, and golden necklace

c). Fine linen clothing

d). An Egyptian wife

e). Ruler of Pharaoh's house

f). Second chariot commander

13. Joseph fathered two sons in Egypt. Name them, and translation of their names, (Gen 41:50-52).

14. How did Jacob bless Joseph and his two sons? (Gen 48:1-22).

15. Find a New Testament reference to Joseph in Egypt.

~ Notes ~

[1] Unger, Merrill F., *The New Unger's Bible Dictionary*. 1988, pg710.
[2] *Firefighter Cassette Tape Series*. Chuck Missler, Genesis 30, 1994
[3] Hammurabi Code, from www.avalon.law.yale.edu
[4] *The King James Study Bible*. Thomas Nelson Inc. 1988, Genesis 11:31
[5] www.blueletterbible.org
[6] ibid

~ 14 ~

JOSEPH, Part II

Lesson Background: Genesis 41-45
Lesson Scriptures: Various

"And Joseph was thirty years old when he stood before Pharaoh king of Egypt. And Joseph went out from the presence of Pharaoh, and went throughout all the land of Egypt." (Gen 41:46, KJV).

When Pharaoh made Joseph second in command of Egypt, Joseph was thirty years old. He came to Egypt as a slave at age seventeen. Now he commanded the second chariot of Pharaoh, and was governor over all the land. Pharaoh had lifted Joseph from the melancholy of prison life to the elegance of palace living. Eventually, Joseph was given the honor, and great responsibility of managing a great nation.

Pharaoh was relieved that Joseph could provide him with the answer to his dreams. He delighted in all that Joseph did, and continued to make various changes in Joseph's life, giving him a new name and a wife—the daughter of the priest of On, a city in lower Egypt.[1] Joseph's new name was Zaphnathpaaneah; his wife was Asenath. They became parents of two sons, Ephraim and Manasseh.

Joseph's work was cut out for him, and he was just the man for the task. God was with him, as he had been in everything Joseph set out to do.

Famine was forecast as God showed Joseph in interpreting the Pharaoh's dreams. However, Egypt would be ready because they now had seven years to prepare. Joseph put his plans into action to ensure the land would have enough food to survive the famine. They knew that seven bad years would follow the seven good ones they enjoyed at the present. God had caused the land to produce so much grain it could not be measured.

The famine came as predicted, however, there was plenty food in Egypt. Surrounding cities heard of the excess in Egypt and came to trade. People bartered all kinds of goods for food, even their servitude. Jacob's family was one of those who came seeking food. When they arrived, the brothers bowed down their faces to the ground before the man in charge, calling him 'my lord'.

Joseph recognized them right away. They understandably did not know him as their brother. He disguised himself as much as possible, speaking roughly to them in the Egyptian tongue. He accused them of spying, and demanded they prove themselves by returning to Canaan and bringing back their younger brother, Benjamin. Joseph put them in prison for three days, choosing one to remain there while the others returned to Canaan. This he demanded; it was not to be negotiated.

Reuben, the eldest, remembered how they had treated Joseph years earlier, even lying to their father about his disappearance. Guilt nagged at his heart as he remembered the anguish of Joseph pleading with them—as they were now imploring this man.

After their return with Benjamin, Joseph put them thru more tests until he was satisfied of their trustworthiness. Believing that they were sorry for selling him into slavery, he revealed who he really was. Some fear, some trembling; some anger, some guilt; some happiness, some tears. Finally, they all made peace with one another, as Joseph explained, 'you meant evil against me, but God meant it for good', (Gen 50:20). After that, Joseph extended Pharaoh's invitation for his entire family to come live in Egypt. They would have the best part of the land in Goshen.

Lesson Discussion: Various Scriptures

1a. Joseph was thirty years old when he became governor of Egypt. How long had he been in Egypt by that time?

1b. Name a New Testament reference of a thirty-year-old leader. Who was he, and what was his mission?

2. Deliberate the fact that Pharaoh indicated recognition of the God of Joseph, (Gen 41:38-39).

3a. Pharaoh recognized the importance of his new commander to have a wife. Discuss thoughts on Pharaoh giving Joseph another man's daughter to marry, (Gen 41:45).

3b. Joseph's wife was not from neither Canaan nor his forefathers' homeland. Discuss implications.

3c. Pharaoh gave Joseph an Egyptian name. How often is that name used as reference to Joseph?

4a. When Joseph's brothers came to Egypt for food, what part of his dreams forecast their actions in bowing down to him?

4b. What can you surmise from Joseph's dreams of eleven sheaves, the sun, and the moon, bowing to his sheaf? (See Gen 37:5-10).

5a. Joseph recognized his brothers right away. Why did he conceal his identity? (Gen 42:7-9; 42:21-23).

5b. In Genesis 42:18, Joseph offered an important clue about himself. Discuss the meaning of that remark.

6a. The money Joseph's brothers brought with them on their original trip for food had not been kept by the Egyptians. What happened? (Gen 42:25-28).

6b. Site several reasons why Joseph insisted Benjamin come to Egypt.

6c. Judah persuaded his father to allow Benjamin to go to Egypt. What convinced Jacob?

7. These buyers from Canaan received very special treatment from the governor of Egypt. Describe the dinner which Joseph had prepared.

8. After repeated tests, Joseph allowed himself to trust his brothers. He told them who he was. Describe what followed, (Gen 45:1-15).

9a. Joseph asked his family to move to Egypt. What reasons did he have for wanting them there? (Gen 45:5-11).

9b. Discuss the choice of Goshen for Joseph's family, (Gen 45:10-11; 47:13).

10a. How many years had it been since Joseph and his father had seen each other? (Gen 37:2; 41:46; 45:6; 47:28-30; 50:26).

10b. Research how many years Jacob and his father Isaac were separated.

~ Notes ~

[1] www.blueletterbible.org

~ 15 ~

JOSEPH, Part III

Lesson Background: Genesis 41-50
Lesson Scriptures: Various

"Now therefore be not grieved, nor angry with yourselves, that ye sold me hither: for God did send me before you to preserve life. ... and to save your lives by a great deliverance." (Gen 45:5, 7, KJV).

Joseph sent word to his father to come to Egypt. He wanted to be sure that all his family could survive the remaining five years of the famine. When Pharaoh heard about Joseph's family, he agreed that they should relocate to Egypt. It pleased Pharaoh to have Joseph run his empire. It pleased Pharaoh to make sure Joseph was satisfied about his father and brothers and all his family. Pharaoh provided food for their round-trip journey to Canaan and back. He also gave them wagons for transporting their families and possessions back to Egypt, and promised them the best of the land, (Gen 45:1-20).

Jacob, the patriarch of the tribes, was not only the father of Israel, his name was changed to Israel when he wrestled with an unknown; a man-angel; the LORD. Who else had authority to change Jacob's name? Jacob acknowledged this man as God. God confirmed Jacob's new name when He reconfirmed the land covenant promised to Abraham, and to Isaac, and to Jacob, (Gen 32:24-30; 35:9-12).

In scripture, the father of Israel is sometimes called Israel, and sometimes he is called Jacob. He was the progenitor of the twelve tribes which became known as the nation of Israel. Israel, God's special designation; his spiritual name, signified the nation. Jacob, his personal name, indicated the man. When Jacob decided to go to Egypt, he spoke as Israel, "And Israel said, ...Joseph, my son, is yet alive: I will go and see him before I die, " (Gen 45:28).

Jacob and families prepared for the journey and departed Canaan to go down into Egypt. On his way, he stopped over in Beersheba which had a special meaning to him. Beersheba was named thus by Jacob's grandfather, Abraham, who planted a tamarisk tree and worshiped God there, after a dispute about a well with Abimelech, (Gen 21:25-34). This same place had been special to Jacob's father Isaac, who also had dealings with a king of the Philistines. The LORD had appeared to Isaac at Beersheba, and in re-cognition of and reverence to God, Isaac built an altar and worshipped there, (Gen 26:1-25).

While in Beersheba, the LORD spoke to Jacob in a dream and told him not to fear going into Egypt. Jacob might have been thinking about the stories of his father in Egypt. In any case, God assured Jacob that He would go down with him into Egypt, and would make of him a great nation there. So, Jacob offered sacrifices and continued the journey into Egypt. His sons, and his grandsons; his daughters, and his sons' daughters, his cattle, and all his household went down into Egypt, (Gen 46:1-7).

Joseph—hated by his brothers, on the brink of being murdered, sold into slavery—was now the man whom they all depended on for their livelihood. He came to meet them, welcomed them, and assured them they would have a prime area to live in and call home. For the time being.

When it came to blessing his family, Jacob's portion to Joseph and Joseph's sons exceeded those given to his other sons. Jacob adopted Ephraim and Manasseh, and claimed them as his own, consoling Joseph by ensuring him that he would only claim those two for himself. All future sons of Joseph would be identified by the paternity of their father, (Gen 48:5-6).

Jacob's adoption and blessings of Ephraim and Manasseh entitled them to be identified as tribes of Israel, along with their father. Throughout the remainder of their history, their names would appear in the records of the tribes. Sometimes, both brothers appear in the same tribal listing; other times only one of them is mentioned, along with their father. The order of their inclusion depended on which tribe is omitted at that time: Levi, Dan, or their father, Joseph.

Ephraim was blessed as Joseph's first born, not his brother Manasseh. In addition, his grandfather promised that he, Ephraim, would be greater than Manasseh. Joseph received a double portion above that of his brothers, which were normally reserved for the first born. However, as Reuben had forfeited that right, Joseph was Israel's next choice, (See also Gen 44:27).

Joseph was further blessed as a fruitful nation. His branches, or offspring, were far-reaching, running entirely over the wall. The hating was not over yet, but the mighty God of his father would sustain him, even bringing forth the 'shepherd, the stone of Israel'. The blessings that Jacob spoke would prevail over the blessings of his forefathers. Joseph was to be blessed of heaven, and of the deep, and of the womb, (Gen 49:22-26).

The children of Israel lived in Egypt for many, many years; four hundred thirty years as prophesied. These Canaanite families would become slaves in Egypt before they were delivered from the hardships of Pharaoh's bondage, (Gen 15:13-14; Ex 12:40-51).

Joseph lived to be a hundred and ten years old. Upon his death, he was embalmed and his bones put in a coffin in Egypt, (Gen 50:22-26). When the time came, his bones were carried with God's people out of Egypt, as he had requested; and as he and his father, Israel, had prophesied, (Gen 48:21; 50:24-26; Ex 13:19).

Jacob also died in Egypt. His sons, and a delegation of Egyptians, carried Jacob's body up out of Egypt and buried him in Canaan, in the field of Ephron, which Abraham had purchased as a burying place for his beloved Sarah.

Lesson Discussion: Various Scriptures

1a. Research and discuss a time when God warned Isaac not go down to Egypt. (Gen 26).

1b. How was Isaac blessed by heeding God's request and camping in Gerar?

1c. Abraham had also lived in Egypt. Why did he go there? When did he leave, and why? (Gen 12:1-13:4)

2a. Explore a map of Canaan, Beersheba, and Egypt. Estimate distance from Canaan to Egypt, and the time Jacob's family spent traveling.

2b. The LORD dispelled Jacob's misgivings about Egypt. What transpired? (Gen 46).

3. Joseph's father, and grandfather, and great-grandfather had a special connection with Beersheba. Examine and discuss. (Gen 21:22-34; 26:18-33).
a). Abraham

b). Isaac

c). Jacob

4a. Father and son met again after many years. Describe their reunion. (Gen 46:26-30).

.

4b. How many of Israel's descendants came down to Egypt with him?

4c. Normally, women were not numbered. How many are included in this count?

5a. Pharaoh was agreeable to Joseph's family moving to Egypt. Discuss.

5b. What caused Joseph to believe Pharaoh would agree for his family to live in the area Joseph had chosen for them? (Gen 46:31-34; 47:1-6).

6a. Name the Pharaoh who had lived where Jacob would live. (Gen 47:11). What impact did he have in Egypt?

6b. What did Jacob do when he met Pharaoh? (Gen 47:7-10).

7a. Jacob was _____ years old when he came to Egypt, (Gen 47:9). Discuss.

7b. Jacob lived in Egypt for _____ years, (Gen 47:28).

7c. Jacob's age at his death?

8. Joseph was _____ years old when he was sold to Egypt for 20 silver coins. How does that amount compare with today's money?

9a. Discuss the years Joseph lived in Egypt. How many years were there? (Gen 50:22).

9b. Explain Joseph's special request before he died. How old at death? (Gen 50:25-26).

10a. How long did the children of Israel live in Egypt? (Gen 15:13; Ex 12; Acts 7:6; Gal 3:17).

10b. Describe the kind of life they had there?

10c. When did they leave Egypt? And who helped them leave?

~ Notes ~

~ 16 ~

ISSACHAR, ZEBULUN, BENJAMIN

Various Background & Lesson Scriptures

Issachar:

"And Leah said, 'God hath given me my hire, because I have given my maiden to my husband:' and she called his name Issachar." (Gen 30:18; KJV).

Issachar and Zebulun were the last two sons Leah gave birth to. The translation of Issachar is explained as a *reward*. Reward fits the usage of the word *hire* that Leah used in verse eighteen. Other synonyms for 'hire' are salary, wages, compensation, benefit, worth, even payment of contract. *The King James Study Bible* notations portray Issachar as *he will bring reward*. This same interpretation is found in *Smiths Bible Dictionary*.[1, 2] According to the Blue Letter Bible website, Issachar is pronounced as, (yis-saw-kawr', and translated as *there is recompense*.[3]

At times these two words—reward and recompense—can be used interchangeably, causing some confusion. A reward hints at nice things, pleasant things; a prize in exchange for something given. Then too, a reward can point to 'just rewards' as something unpleasant. On the other hand, a recompense can be interpreted as punishment, or a payment for loss or harm suffered. The word can be used as compensation for payment of damages, or reimbursement for making restitution. Yet, a recompense can also be used to satisfy an expected reward.[4] In your studies, you will discover that word translations always depend heavily upon their relationship to the scenario being narrated.

Even Leah's reasoning in naming Issachar can be translated in several ways. His being conceived might have been a reward for giving Rachel the mandrakes Reuben had brought her. But, she also hired, or paid for Jacob with those mandrakes so he would sleep in her tent that night, (Gen 30:16). However, in reading verse eighteen more closely, Leah might have had an entirely different reason in naming Issachar. Look at the following words: '...because I have given my maiden to my husband.' It seems Leah might have felt rewarded because she had given Zilpah to Jacob to bear children in her place. Zilpah produced two sons: Asher and Naphtali. And then sometime later, Leah conceived again when she thought her childbearing days were over, (Gen 30:14-18). Ergo, her reward.

Issachar, blessed by his father, was associated with a strong ass couching down between two burdens. An ass is a male donkey; slow, patient, strong, and used mainly as a beast of burden.[5, 6] Couching down can be translated as reposing, resting, lurking, or waiting. One explanation of Issachar's association with two burdens refers to a sheepfold which is a stall or enclosure for cattle.

In the Bible, a flock can describe any domestic animal. Sheep are often referred to as sheep, goats, even cattle. Issachar characteristically preferred resting more than working. He deemed rest as an advantage, and during his adventures found himself a servant of tribute. Jacob, however, being blessed with a keen sense of observation and foresight, had predicted it, (Gen 49:14-15). Tribute used here refers to forced service, a labor-gang.[7]

Moses advised Issachar to rejoice in his tents, (Deu 33:18-19). That short five word statement was all Moses had to say in blessing Issachar. And too, Issachar's blessing is combined in the same declarative as that of Zebulun. This is most vague, and could be an indication of Issachar's decision to explore for more. Is he included in *they* of verse nineteen?

Issachar Discussion: Gen 30:14-18; 35:22; 37:2; 49:14-15; Deu 33:18-19

1a. Explain interpretation of hire, and give examples.

1b. When is a reward a recompense? Describe an example.

2a. Look up description of a mandrake. Discuss its uses.

2b. How did Rachel benefit from mandrakes?

2c. Examine the outcome of the mandrakes in this story.

3a. Explain the Gen 30:18 reference 'given my maiden to my husband.'

3b. Were Bilhah and Zilpah considered concubines or wives? Give references.

4a. Name and explain the two burdens predicted for Issachar.

4b. Discuss the beast of burden seen in Issachar's future by his father.

5. How did the 'pleasant lands' cause Issachar misfortune?

6a. Can you envision how Issachar became a servant?

6b. What was the tribute Issachar received?

7. Discuss the blessing of Moses for Issachar to 'rejoice in his tents'. As this is not broadly defined, use imagination.

Zebulun:

"And Leah conceived again, and bare Jacob a sixth son. And Leah said, God hath endued me with a good dowry; now will my husband dwell with me, because I have born him six sons: and she called his name Zebulun." (Gen 30:20, KJV).

Leah considered Zebulun a gift from God, as seen in the words 'good dowry'. Zebulun is pronounced (zeb-oo-loon, as in zev ü lün), translated as *exalted*, and is associated with habitation.[8, 9] One synonym for habitation is *dwelling*. After the birth of Zebulun, Leah hoped that Jacob would be so pleased with her that he would want to *dwell* exclusively in her tent, (Gen 30:20).

Leah gave birth to more sons than any of Jacob's other wives. In fact, she gave birth to three times as many sons as Rachel, or Bilhah, or Zilpah. One can visualize how Leah could expect to be rewarded, even feel entitled to Jacob's affection and time. She also gave birth to Dinah, Jacob's only daughter named in scripture, (Gen 30:21; 46:15). Leah could surely assume her accomplishments as a wife to be exemplary. She expected and received a good dowry; a reward. She expected, and longed for preference in the eyes of her husband.

In Jacob's blessings, Zebulun was fated to dwell near the sea, and be a port for ships. Zebulun's dwelling place bordered Zidon, which is an ancient and wealthy city of Phoenician, or Phenicia. Zidon and Sidon are the same place, spelled differently in various scriptures, (Gen 10:15; 49:13). Just as an aside, according to Blue Letter Bible, the Strong's number H6721 is spelled twenty times as Zidon, and only twice as Sidon.[10]

Sidon is the Greek form of the Phoenician name Zidon which is referred to as Sidon the metropolis, (Gen 10:15; 49:13; Joshua 11:8).[11, 12] The place is considered a good area for fishing, (Gen 49:13; Deu 33:18-19; Acts 21:2). Another interpretation for Zidon or Sidon relates to hunting, which ordinarily refers to finding big game: deer, buffalo, birds, and other beasts of prey. In this sense, one's imagination can be stretched to include hunting, as some big fish are speared. Zidon, or Sidon is pronounced as *tsee-done,* and infers a hunting connotation by Strong's number H6679 as catching fish. [13]

Looking at Deuteronomy's reference in verse nineteen, we find it non-specific as to who the blessing addresses in calling people to the mountain for offering sacrifices. However, we know from Jacob's blessings that Zebulun will benefit from the sea. Moses advises Zebulun to rejoice in his territories from the sea, and of the hidden treasures there.

Zebulun Discussion: Various Scriptures

1a). Define a dowry.

b). What did Leah consider a good dowry?

c). Was Leah's dowry enough to sway Jacob's love away from Rachel?

d). Investigate which of Jacob's wives lived with him the longest.

2. Consider Zebulun as:
a). Exalted

b). An Habitation

3a. Zebulun was predicted to have a port for ships. Where would this port be located? (Gen 49:13).

3b. What kind of treasures could Zebulun expect from the sea?

4. Explore entrepreneurial opportunities to be found in the sand's raw materials.

5. Look at cross-references for Deuteronomy 33:18-19. How do these references add to, or complement, the other verses concerning Zebulun? (Gen 49:13; Jos 19:10-16; Ps 4:5; Jer 50:4-5; others).

Benjamin:

"And Rachel travailed, and she had hard labor....And it came to pass, as her soul was in departing, (for she died) that she called his name Benoni: but his father called him Benjamin." (Gen 35:16-18, KJV).

Benoni was born on the road to Ephrath, between Bethel and Ephrath. Rachel died giving birth to her second son, whom she named as her life was fleeting. This newborn's name accentuated Rachel's extreme pain and agony of her labor. Benoni means 'son of my sorrow', and is pronounced as (ben-ō-nē'), (Gen 35:16-19).

Jacob's actions to rename Benoni as Benjamin indicated his desire for a more satisfying name for his son. One that had a pleasant tone and association; one that would describe who his son was, rather than an inference to his birth. A name that would bring him, Jacob, soothing, rather than haunting thoughts of Rachel's painful death.

For Jacob, Benjamin, which means 'son of my right hand', is perfectly understandable and preferred to Benoni, and 'son of my sorrow'. Neither would he want his son to grow up feeling guilty about his mother's dying as he was born. Benjamin is pronounced as (bin yä mene'). This was the only son whom Jacob named. The other eleven sons were named by either Leah or Rachel.

After his birth, Benjamin is not mentioned again until the tribes went to Egypt in search of food, (Gen 42:4). At the time, Joseph was governor, and insisted that Benjamin come to Egypt as proof of his brothers' claims that they were not spies. Probably, Joseph also wanted desperately to see his younger brother, and have comfort in knowing that Benjamin yet lived, as well as his father. (Gen 42:4-43:34).

Jacob's blessing to Benjamin foresees him as a ravenous wolf, capturing his prey during the morning, and dividing the spoil at night, (Gen

49:27). This speaks of ferocious strength; plundering, merciless, and predatory; painting Benjamin as a force to deal with. He would be a strong, fierce tribe equipped to protect, and provide for the family.

Moses' blessing for Benjamin was for safety and continual protection. Moses was certain that the LORD would always be with Benjamin; and provide him protection and safety all day long. The LORD would surely dwell between his shoulders, (Deu 33:12).

Benjamin Discussion: Gen 35:16-19; 42:4-43:34; 49:27; Deu 33:12
1. Define the word 'travail' which is used frequently throughout the Bible.

2. Consider reasons for Benjamin's parents in naming him.
a). Rachel:

b). Jacob:

3a. Locate Benjamin's birth place on a Bible map, and discuss.

3b. What are original names of nearby towns mentioned, and their modern-day names?

3c. What could cause Jacob to travel with Rachel so close to childbirth?

4. Both mother and/or father named children in the Bible; at times following God's directive, or those communicated by an angel. Discuss Jacob's children being named by his wives, Leah and Rachel.

5. Benjamin's future predicted: fierceness, destruction, and violence. Discuss positives and negatives of these character traits.
a). Fierceness

b). Destruction

c). Violence

6. How does the blessing of Moses for Benjamin impact the blessing of Jacob?

7. Examine the demands of Joseph to 'see Benjamin' as a condition of selling food to his brothers.

8. Imagine the scene when Joseph surrendered his emotions to tears. What could have gone through his brothers' minds?

9. How did Joseph respond upon learning that his father was alive?

10. What was the tribes native tongue and what language did Joseph use in speaking to his brothers?

11a. Discuss Joseph's reasons for wanting his family in Egypt. (Gen 47).

11b. On the way down to Egypt, Jacob made a stop. Where? Why?

11c. How long did he stay in that place?

12. Name a New Testament relative of Benjamin's.

Issachar, Zebulun, Benjamin—Rank and Numbers

Numbers chapter one shows the total qualifying men of **Issachar's** tribe as 54,400. In Numbers chapter two, Issachar was designated a camp position with Judah, and Zebulun, (Num 2:7-9). The tribal numbers of Issachar near Jericho, in the plains of Moab, totaled 64,300, (Num 26:25). Issachar's allotment of the new land was determined in the fourth lot cast, (Jos 19:17-23).

Numbers chapter two determines **Zebulun** as having a camp station on the east of the Levites and the tabernacle. Their position faced the rising sun, in the same camp, and following the same marching order as Judah and **Issachar**, (Num 2:7-9).

Originally, **Zebulun's** tribe totaled 57,400 men strong, (Num 1; 2). As they prepared to receive their inheritance, their numbers were 60,500, (See Num 26:26-27). The lot for their families was the third chosen; their land bordered Sarid, the chief landmark of Zebulun. The translation of Sarid is *survivor*, and borders on Palestine, (Jos 19:10-16).[14]

Benjamin's assigned station aligned his tribe alongside Ephraim and Manasseh, (Num 2:18-24). In the wilderness of Sinai, Benjamin's tribe equaled 35,400 men, (Num 1:37). In Moab, near the Jordan crossing, they numbered 45,600; and their lot was determined first in the distribution of the promised land, (Num 2:22-23; 26:41; Jos 18:10-28).

Jacob's family going into Egypt established **Issachar's** tribe with four sons. They were Tola, Phuvah, Job, and Shimron, (Gen 46:13). **Zebulun** brought three sons: Sered, Elon, and Jahleel, (Gen 46:14). **Benjamin** had ten sons: Belah, Becher, Ashbel, Gera, Naaman, Ehi, Rosh, Muppim, Huppim, and Ard, (Gen 46:21).

Leaving Canaan for Egypt with Jacob were his children, along with their children, totaling sixty-six people. Joseph was already in Egypt, with his two sons. Including Jacob, this accounts for a total of seventy Israelites in Egypt at that time of Genesis forty-six.

Seventy souls traveled into Egypt originally, and approximately 3,200,000 came out of Egypt during their Exodus. This conservative number allows for wives and children of the men counted while they were in the wilderness of Sinai. At that time, the count was 603,550 men, (Num 1:46). One wife per war-ready prince adds 603,550 women. Three children per couple would add another 1,810,650 people.* Considering these numbers, there could well have been over 3,000,000 people strong coming out of Egypt. (See examples below).*

These illustrated examples total 3,017,750 people. This doesn't account for unmarried women, men under twenty years old, strangers born among them, nor servants that might have joined Israel while they were in Egypt.

*Example count of families:
1,207,100 (adding one wife per 603,550 princes).
1,810,650 (3 children per couple; 3 is arbitrary number. I'm sure there were more children for some couples; choose your own number and do the math.
3,017,750 (total men, wives, and three children families).
3,200,000 plus when including: married men less than age 20; unmarried women; strangers born among them, and children not counted in the example of 3 children per couple.

Rank and Numbers Discussion: Various Scriptures
1. Observe the number of Issachar, Zebulun, and Benjamin during the first and the last tribal count. What can you draw from their numbers?

2. Explain importance of:

a). The Jordan River

b). Land east of the Jordan

c). Land west of the Jordan

d). Significance of the count before crossing the river

3. Which tribes chose land east of the Jordan, and what convinced them to settle there?

4. Name the tribes who established homesteads west of the Jordan.

5. One tribe was hardly ever listed with their brothers.
a). Who were they? Discuss their status.

b). Do you think that tribe was treated unfairly? Why? Or why not?

6. Discuss Israel's numbers as they migrated out of Egypt.

7. Consider their numbers going into their promised territory after forty years of weariness, hardship, and heartbreak in getting there. What are your thoughts?

8. Moses had his hands full leading over 1,600,000 people out of Egypt. (This number estimates women and children.) After a time, Moses had seventy judges to help him manage such a huge following. Who assisted Joshua with the 3,000,000 plus people going into Canaan?

~ Notes ~

[1] The King James Study Bible, Genesis 30:18
[2] Smith, William L.L.D., Smith's Bible Dictionary, Thomas Nelson, 1986, p. 271
[3] www.blueletterbible.org (blb); Strong's word connection; Genesis 30:18
[4] Microsoft Word Smart Lookup
[5] ibid, blb; Strong's word connection; Genesis 49:14
[6] Dictionary.com
[7] ibid, blb; Strong's word connection; Genesis 49:14-15
[8] ibid, blb; Strong's word connection; Genesis 30:20
[9] ibid, blb; Strong's word connection; Genesis 49:13; Joshua 19:10
[10] ibid, blb; Strong's word connection; Genesis 10:15
[11] ibid, Smith's Bible Dictionary, p. 628
[12] ibid, blb; Gen 10:15; 49:13; Joshua 11:8
[13] ibid, blb; Strong's word connection; Genesis 49:13
[14] ibid, Smith; p. 591

~ 17 ~

Dig Deep, Aim High

Challenge Section
Various Scriptures

"Study to shew thyself approved unto God, a workman that needeth not to be ashamed, rightly dividing the word of truth...Search the scriptures...they are they which testify of me." (2 Tim 2:15; Jhn 5:39; KJV).

The history of the tribes of Israel is interspersed throughout the Bible. Information in this book relates mainly to their background in Genesis, and their migration to the promise of an inheritance recorded in the Torah. Even that information is a synopsis of their travels; omitting the many battles along the way; the struggles for power and survival; the kingships of their generations; the splitting of the tribes, and many other events.

Because this book is an abridgment of the tribes' activities, I invite you to dig into God's Word a little deeper. Dare your mind to grasp more. Seek and investigate the layers beneath the surface of what's written in a single scripture. Explore the background of numerous imprecise verses; the seemingly out of sequence or stand-alone scriptures; and those complex scenarios, which may or may not relate to other events in the Bible.

Aim high. Allow your awareness to be lifted higher and higher. Let His Spirit guide you to a greater understanding of what He inspired to be written. Dig Deep to gain wisdom. The more you saturate your taste, the hungrier you will be for his Word. Wisdom is the fundamental thing, worth more than gold, and often used side by side with understanding. Your cup will be running over with joy, enlightenment, understanding, enthusiasm, knowledge, and wisdom. (Proverbs 4:5,7; 7:4; 16:16; Job 28:12-15).

As David said to his son Solomon, "Only the LORD give thee wisdom and understanding...," (1 Chronicles 22:12). And Job; "And unto man he [God] said, Behold, the fear of the Lord, that is wisdom; and to depart from evil is understanding," (Job 28:28).

In all you do, get an understanding, (Proverbs 4:7).

Challenge Questions:

I. **About the Bible: Various**

1. Explore the following:

a). Original language of Old Testament? New Testament?

b). Native language(s) of Israel?

c). Research 'King James' of the King James Version of the Bible.

d). Which languages were involved in translating the King James Bible?

e). Which Bible translation is your favorite? Why?

II. About Israel's Ancestors: Various Genesis Verses, Chapters 10-27

1. Which son of Noah was progenitor of Israel? Name your references.

2. Why was Israel chosen to be God's special people? Name references.

3. Who was the recognized *original* father of Israel's people? Use any reference.

4. Where did this man live when God captured his attention, and of what nationality or culture was he? List references.

5. God required much of this man. What promises did God make? List references.

6. Why is it not descriptive enough to describe God's promise as preordained for Abraham's descendants? List references.

7. Where did Isaac and Jacob originally live? List references.

8. How did Israel end up in Egypt? (Gen 45-50).

9. How long did Israel live as slaves in Egypt? (Gen 15:13; Ex 12:40-41; Acts 7:6; Gal 3:17).

10. Which of Israel's ancestors (other than Jacob and Joseph), had lived in Egypt during their life-time? Why? List references.

III. About Journey to New Land: (Ex 2-12; Deu 1); Give References
1. Where was Moses when God chose him to lead Israel out of Egypt?

2. How did God show His power through Moses? List references.

3a. Moses led Israel three days out of Egypt after crossing the Red Sea. Discuss reasons for their first stop, and other circumstances. Your choice of references.

3b. Map their journey in distance and time from Egypt to where God instructed Israel to go. List references.

4a. Examine God's choice of land promised to Israel. List references.

4b. Who were the people who lived in that territory at that time? Use any reference you choose.

4c. What did Israel have to do to live in their new land? List references.

5. Why would God take land from people who already lived there, and give it to Israel? List references.

6a. Review the advance party Moses sent to scout the land, (Num 13).

6b. Name each tribe and representative Moses dispatched to evaluate the countryside. List references.

7. Two scouts believed Israel could prevail against their enemy nations; ten did not. Name the men, their tribes; and their recommendations to Moses. Discuss what transpired because of their beliefs. List references.

8. How long did it take Israel to accomplish their goal of occupying this land God had promised? Why? List references.

9. Great-great-great-great-granddaughters of Joseph were first women to inherit land. What was their situation? (Jos 17:1-4).

10. Discuss deaths of Moses and Aaron. Where did each die? Why? When? List references.

IV. Historical Listings of the Tribes: Various

1a. Investigate three scripture references where the tribes are listed in a different order. Compare the names; discuss who is omitted from each list, and give references.

1b. Annotate translation of each tribal name as it appears in your lists. Your observations? Name your references.

2. Look at the periodic change in tribal listings. Name the tribe most often omitted, and your thoughts on why? List references.

3a. There are always twelve tribes listed at any one time. Can you validate this?

3b. Contemplate the implication of thirteen, even fourteen tribes. When could this have been a relevant option? List references.

4. Many great leaders evolved from the tribes of Israel. Name three men from each of following categories. List references.
a). Prophet:

b). King:

c). Apostle:

5. Israel had the smallest number of people of any nation when God chose them to be His representatives. The greatest king came from their smallest city or town. Name him, and his birthplace. (Micah 5:2).

V. **Defending the Tabernacle: Various**

1. Whether stationary, or moving, Levi family members encircled the Tabernacle of the Congregation. Judah guarded eastern borders; Ephraim guarded western borders; Dan guarded norther borders; and Reuben guarded the south. Sketch a word picture of their positions.

2. Describe what your portrayal of Israel's camp[1] reveals to you?

VI. **About The Split Kingdoms; Give References**

1. Which tribes were included in the Northern Kingdom, known as Israel? (Hint: Search for: house of Judah, or house of Israel; or Northern and Southern kingdom. 2Sam 2-5; 12; 1Ki 11; 12:15-23; 20-21:18; 22:1-44; 1Chr 28:4; 2Chr 11:1; other references).

2. Name several kings of the Northern Kingdom. Suggest you search on kings of Israel. Name your references.

3. There were times when the Northern Kingdom and the Southern Kingdom were both referred to by the name of a single tribe. Which tribes were those? Discuss your thoughts on the matter. List references.

4. Name several kings of the Southern Kingdom. Name the tribes which comprised that kingdom. Search on kings of Judah, and give references.

5. What is indicative of the term, 'from Dan to Beersheba'? List references.

6. What have you observed, and learned in this study of Israel's tribes?

7. Do you feel a particular kinship to any one of the tribes? How so?

8. Even with the force and assurance of God with them, Israel did not drive out their enemies. They won many battles, when they followed God's instructions. They lost many more when they ignored His instructions. What have you lost by not following God's commands?

VII. Assorted Information and Interesting Facts

1a. What name was Joseph given by a pharaoh of Egypt? Reference?

1b. How is that name translated in Hebrew? In Egyptian? Reference?

1c. Why do you think the name was never repeated in scripture?

2. How old was Joseph when he was elevated to Pharaoh's second in command? References?

3a. Research the significance of age thirty for Jewish leaders. Give examples of several of those leaders. References?

3b. What seems to be the appropriate characteristics of age thirty?

4. Deliberate the prominence of Pharaohs and Kings. What distinguishes one from the other? References?

5a. Name the jewels required to be embedded in the robes of Levitical priests. (Exo 28).

5b. Name the jewels in the foundation of the jasper walls of New Jerusalem? (Rev 21:18-20).

6a. Compare the jewels of the priests' robes with the jewels of the new city foundations. List reference.

6b. Along with the bejeweled foundation in Revelation, there is another place of honor on each foundation. Who will be esteemed in all that brilliance? References?

7a. The new city of Jerusalem will have twelve pearly gates. Along with an angel at each gate, who else will be exemplified there? References?

7b. How can you determine which names will appear on these gates?

8. Who will guard the gates? Expound on your answer. Reference?

9. Describe the Temple found in the New Jerusalem. Reference?

10. How are you preparing to enjoy that glorious light of Heaven?

~ Notes ~

[1] Missler, Chuck; *The Camp of Israel.* (Koinonia House Ministries, 1993).

Reference Tables

God…, Adam to Noah

Some Information Repeated
For Ease of Correlation

Genesis 9:18-10:32

©tjjohnson, 2004

I
GOD

*References: [1] [2] [3]

Name	Translation	Age of Father*	Other Info.
GOD Elōhīym (el-o-heem')	The Godhead, Rulers, Judges		Plural Majesty
II. Adam (aw-dawm')	Man, mankind		First man; father of humankind
Eve (khav-vaw') Woman (ish-shaw')	Life/living; From man		Woman; Eve; mother of all

*Father's age at birth of son used throughout; references 1-3 used throughout

II-Adam

Name	Translation	Age of Father	Other Info.
Adam (aw-dawm')	Man, mankind		First man; father of humankind; lived to be 930 yrs. old
a. **Cain** (kah'-yin)	Acquire; Possession		Tiller of the ground; Killed his brother because of envy, Gen 4:1-8
b. **Abel** (heh'-bel)	Breath; Keeper		Keeper of sheep

c. **Seth** (shayth)	Appointed; Compensation	*Adam 130	Seth lived to be 912 yrs. old
d. Other sons & daughters			Gen 5:4

Adan 130yrs at birth of Seth

IIa. Adam-Cain

Name	Translation	Age of Father	Other Info.
Cain (kah'-yin) & wife	Acquire; Possession		Tilled the ground; Killed his brother
1. Enoch (khan-oke')	Dedicated, Initiated		Cain built a city named after Enoch

IIa. Cain-Enoch

Name	Translation	Age of Father	Other Info.
Enoch (khan-oke') & wife	Dedicated, Initiated		
1. Irad (ee-rawd')	Fleet		

IIa. Cain-Irad

Name	Translation	Age of Father	Other Info.
Irad (ee-rawd')			
1. Mehujael (mekh-oo-yaw-ale')	Smitten by God		

IIa. Irad-Mehujael

Name	Translation	Age of Father	Other Info.
Mehujael			
1. Methusael (meth-oo-shaw-ale')	Who is of God		

IIa. Mehujael-Methusael

Name	Translation	Age of Father	Other Info.
Methusael (meth-oo-shaw-ale')	Who is of God		
1. Lamech (leh'-mek)	Powerful		

IIa. Methusael-Lamech & Adah

Name	Translation	Age of Father	Other Info.
Lamech (leh'-mek) **& Adah** (aw-daw')	Powerful Ornament		Gen 4:19-22
1. Jabal (yaw-bawl')			Father of tent dwellers, and livestock owners
2. Jubal (yoo-bawl')			Father of harp and flute musicians

IIa. Methusael-Lamech & Zillah

Name	Translation	Age of Father	Other Info.
Lamech(leh'-mek) **& Zillah** (tsil-law')	Powerful Shade		
1. Tubal-cain (too-bal' kah'-yin)	Thou will be brought of Cain		Craftsman in brass and iron
2. Naamah (nah-am-aw')	loveliness		A daughter

IIc. Adam-Seth

Name	Translation	Age of Father	Other Info.
c. Seth (shayth)	Appointed; Compensation		Seth lived 912 yrs. Begat other sons and daughters
Enos (Ē'nŏs)	A man	*Seth 105yrs	

IIc. Seth-Enos

Name	Translation	Age of Father	Other Info.
Enos (Ē'nŏs)	A man		Lived to 905 yrs. Begat other sons and daughters
Cainan (kay-nawn')	Possession	*Enos 90yrs	

IIc. Enos-Cainan

Name	Translation	Age of Father	Other Info.
Cainan (kay-nawn')	Possession	was 70 at son's birth	Lived to 910 yrs Begat other sons and daughters
Mahalaleel (mah-hal-al-ale')	Praise of God		

IIc. Cainan-Mahalaleel

Name	Translation	Age of Father	Other Info.
Mahalaleel (mah-hal-al-ale')	Praise of God	was 65 at son's birth	Lived to 895 yrs Begat other sons and daughters
Jared (yeh'-red)	Descent		

IIc. Mahalaleel-Jared

Name	Translation	Age of Father	Other Info.
Jared (yeh'-red)	Descent	Was 162 yrs. at son's birth	Lived to 962 yrs. Begat other sons and daughters
Enoch (khan-oke')	Dedicated, Initiated		

IIc. Jared-Enoch

Name	Translation	Age of Father	Other Info.
Enoch (khan-oke')	Dedicated	65yrs at son's birth	Lived to 365 yrs. Begat other sons and daughters
Methuselah (meth-oo-sheh'-lakh)	Man of the javelin		

IIc. Enoch-Methuselah

Name	Translation	Age of Father	Other Info.
Methuselah (meth-oo-sheh'-lakh)	Man of the javelin	187yrs at son's birth	Lived 969 yrs. Begat other sons and daughters
Lamech (leh'-mek)	Powerful		

IIc. Methuselah-Lamech

Name	Translation	Age of Father	Other Info.
Lamech (leh'-mek)	Powerful	182 at son's birth	Lived to be 777 yrs. old. Begat other sons and daughters
Noah	Rest or comfort		He shall comfort us concerning our work & toil of the ground

~ Notes ~

Majority of Table information comes from these main sources

[1] The King James Study Bible, Thomas Nelson, 1988
[2] www.Blueletterbible.org, (most name & word translations)
[3] Unger's Bible Dictionary, Moody Press, 1981

Reference Tables for:

Noah, Ham (II), and Japheth (III),
And Descendants

Some Information Repeated
For Ease of Correlation

Genesis 10:1-30

Noah's Sons

Name	Translation	Age of Father	Other Info.
<u>Noah</u>	Rest or comfort	500 Gen 5:32	Had grace
I. *Shem (shěm)	name, renown		Father of Semitics
II. Ham (hăm) Fathered Canaanites	hot		Libya, Ethiopia, Egypt,
III. Japheth (jā' feth)	opened, God will enlarge		Europe & Asia

*(I. Shem charts shown extensively and separately, beginning on pg. 94)

II. Ham

Name	Translation	Age of Father	Other Info.
<u>Ham</u> (hăm) Father of Canaanites; Begat sons:	Hot		Father of Libya, Canaanites; Egyptians; Ethiopia
a. **Cush** (koosh)	Black		Grandson of Noah, progenitor of southernmost peoples of Africa, near the Nile (Ethiopia):Ez. 38:5
b. **Mizraim** (mits-rah'-yim)	Land of the Copts		Northeastern Africa, adjacent to Palestine where the Nile flows; natives of Egypt

c. **Phut/Put** (poot)	A Bow		People of Libya; Ez. 38:5
d. **Canaan** (ken-ah'-an)	Lowland		Progenitor of the Phoenicians and of seacoast of Palestine

II. Ham-a.
Cush

Name	Translation	Age of Father	Other Info.
a. <u>**Cush**</u> (koosh)	Black		Grandson of Noah & father southern Africa, near Nile (Ethiopia)
1. Seba (seb-aw')	Drink thou		A nation south of Palestine
2. Havilah (khav-ee-law')	Circle		District in Arabia of the Ishmaelite
3. Sabtah (sab-taw')	Unknown		
4. <u>Raamah</u> (rah-maw')	Horse's mane		
5. Sabtechan (sab-tē-aw')	Striking		
6. **Nimrod** (nim-rode')	Let us revolt;[1] vailiant[2] or rebel[3]		Rebel leader, Babel the launch of his kingdoms, Gen 11:1-9; Nimrod could've been leader.

II. Ham-a.4
Ramaah

Name	Translation	Age of Father	Other Info.
4. Raamah (rah-maw')	Horse's mane		
Sheba (sheb-aw')	Seven; an oath		Arabian people NW. of Persian Gulf.[4]
Dedan (ded-awn')	Low country		

II. Ham-a.6
Nimrod

Name	Translation	Age of Father	Other Info.
6. Nimrod			Kingdoms
Babel (baw-bel')	Confusion by mixing		The ancient site and/or capital of Babylonia (modern Hillah) situated on the Euphrates
Erech (eh'-rek)	Long		A city 40 miles (64 km) northwest of Ur toward Babylon on the left bank of the Euphrates river
Accad (ak-kad')	Stubble		City in north Babylonia, and the district around it
Calneh (kal-neh')	Fortress of Anu		Of Shinar. ancient Babylonia or Chaldea

Nineveh (nee-nev-ay')	Abode of Ninus		In the land of Assyria
Rehoboth (rekh-o-both')	Wide places		
Calah (keh'-lakh)	Vigor		Capital of Assyria; east bank Tigris
Resen (reh'-sen)	Bridle		Assyria between Nineveh and Calah

II. Ham-b.
Mizraim

Name	Translation	Age of Father	Other Info.
b. Mizraim (mits-rah'-yim)	Egypt; land of the Copts		NE of Africa, near Palestine and Nile area; Egyptian
1. Ludim (loo-dee')	Travailing		
2. Anamim (an-aw-meem')	Affliction of the waters		
3. Lehabim (leh-haw-beem')	Flames		
4. Naphtuhim (naf-too-kheem)	Opening		
5. Pathrusim (path-roo-see')	Pathros, region of the south		Of Egypt; Is 11:11;
6. **Casluhim** (kas-loo'-kheem)	Fortified		Of the Philistines and Caphtorim
7. Caphtorim (kaf-to-ree')	Caphtor, crown		Cretans of Caphtor, distinct from the Philistines

II. Ham-b.6
Casluhim

Name	Translation	Age of Father	Other Info.
6. **Casluhim** begat (kas-loo'-kheem)	Fortified		Progenitors of the Philistines and Caphtorim
Philistim (pel-ish-tee')	Immigrants		Of Philistia; Mizraim; and Caphtor

II. Ham-d.
Canaan

Name	Translation	Age of Father	Other Info.
d. **Canaan** (ken-ah'-an) Son of Ham, fathered Phoenicians & others	Lowland		Of Ham, fathered Phoenicians, & nations of seacoast Palestine
1. Sidon/Zidon (tsee-done')	Hunting		Phoenician city, north coast of Tyre
2. Heth (khayth)	Terror		Progenitor of the Hittites
3. Jubsite/Jebus (yeb-oo-see')	Descendants of Jebus		Jebus, later Jerusalem
4. Amorite (em-o-ree')	A sayer		East Canaan and dispossessed by the Israelites

5. Girgasite (ghir-gaw-shee')	Dwells on clay soil		East of the sea of Galilee when the Israelites entered
6. Hivite (khiv-vee')	Villagers		N. Canaan near Mt Hermon at the time of conquest
7. Arkite (ar-kee')	Gnawing		Inhabitant of Arki or Arka
8. Sinite (see-nee')	Thorn or Clay		N. Lebanon
9. Arvadite (ar-vaw-dee')	I shall break loose		
10. Zemarite (tsem-aw-ree')			
11. Hamathite (kham-aw-thee')	Fortress[3]		Ancient capital of upper Syria.[3]

III. Japheth

Name	Translation	Age of Father	Other Info.
Japheth (jā' feth)	opened, God will enlarge		Coastal peoples; went North to Europe & Asia
a. **Gomer** (go'-mer)	Complete		Father of the early Cimmerians and other Celtics

b. Magog (maw-gogue')	Land of Gog		Lydians, Scythians, Tartars[4]
c. Madai (maw-dah'-ee)	Media, Middle lands		Medes, same area as modern Iran
d. Javan (yaw-vawn')	Ionia or Greece		Greece
e. Tubal (too-bal')	He shall be brought		Eastern Asia Minor
f. f. Meshech (meh'-shek)	Drawing out; tall		Of Russian, Slavic peoples.[4]
g. Tiras (tee-rawce')	Desire		

III. Japheth-a.
Gomer

Name	Translation	Age of Father	Other Info.
a. Gomer (go'-mer)	Complete		Father of the early Cimmerians and other Celts
Ashkenaz (ash-ken-az')	A man sprinkled; scattered fire		Assyrians, Scythians[3]; Associated with Ararat (Jer 51:27)[4]
Riphath (ree-fath')	Spoken		
Togarmah (to-gar-maw')	Thou will break her		Of the far north[5] followers of Gog

~ Notes ~

[1] The King James Study Bible, Thomas Nelson, 1988
[2] www.Blueletterbible.org
[3] Unger's Bible Dictionary, Moody Press, 1981
[4] The New Compact Bible Dictionary, Zondervan Publishing House, 1967
[5] The King James Study Bible, Thomas Nelson, 1988, Ez. 38:2

Table References For:

Shem (I), Terah, Abram,
Sarah, and Isaac

Noah Table Repeated
For Ease of Correlation

Genesis 10:22-32; 11:10-30

Noah's Sons

(Chart repeated for ease of association; Ham charts pgs.86-90; Japheth charts begin pg.91)

Name	Translation	Age of Father	Other Info.
Noah	Rest or comfort		Had grace in
I. *__Shem__ (shĕm)	name, renown	500 yrs. Gen 5:32	Father of Semitics
II. **Ham** (hăm)	hot		Father of Libya, Canaanites; Ethiopia, Egypt
III. **Japheth** (jā' feth)	opened, God will enlarge		Coastline peoples; went North to Europe & Asia

I. Shem

Name	Translation	Age of Father	Other Info.
Shem (shĕm)	Gen 11:10	Lived to age 600	other sons and daughters
a. Elam (ē' lăm)	eternity		
b. Asshur (ăsh' ûr)	step	(Gen 10:11)	Assyria; built Nineveh, Rehoboth, Calah, Resen[1]
c. **Arphaxad** (är-făx' ăd)	born 2 yrs. after the flood (Gen. 11:11)	Shem 100 at birth of Arphaxad	Forefather of Abraham, others[2]
d. Lud (lŭd)	strife		Of Lydia; N. Africa

e. **Aram** (ăʹrɑ̆m)	exalted; means Syria, also Mesopotamia[3] (Judges 3:10; 3:6)	(Gen 25:20; Deu. 26:5) [4]	Arameans of Phoenicia, Syria is (short for Assyria); Mesopotamia; Seleucid; Aramaic; Rebekah's ancestry[4]

I. Shem-c. Arphaxad

Name	Translation	Age of Father	Other Info.
c. **Arphaxad** (är-făxʼ ăd)		Lived to age 438	Ancestor of Abram, sons & daug., Arabs
1. **Salah**, (sāʼ lɑ̆) shehʼ-lakh,	Missile, javelin, (Shelah)/sprout	35 yrs at son's birth	Gen 11

I. Shem-c1. Salah

Name	Translation	Age of Father	Other Info.
1. **Salah** (sāʼ lɑ̆)		Lived to age 433	other children
Eber, Heber, or Ebet (ēʼ bêr)	other side of the river	Salah 30 yrs.	*said to be the founder of Hebrews*

I. Shem-c1-1.
Eber

Name	Translation	Age of Father	Other Info.
1. **Eber**	region beyond; immigrant	Lived to age 464	other sons and daughters
a. **Peleg,** (pē' lĕg)	Division	Eber 34 yrs.	The earth was divided in his day
b. **Joktan** (jŏk' tăn)	Smallness		patriarch of Arabia

I. Shem-c1-1a.
Eber Peleg

Name	Translation	Age of Father	Other Info.
a. **Peleg** (pē' lĕg)	Division	Lived to age 239	other sons and daughters
Reu (rē' ū)	Friendship	Peleg 30 yrs.	Ragau in Luke 3:35

I. Shem-c1-1a.
Peleg-Reu

Name	Translation	Age of Father	Other Info.
Reu	Friendship	Lived to age 239	Other sons and daughters
Serug (sē'rŭg)	shoot or tendril	Reu 32 yrs.	Saruch Lu. 3:35, Mesopotamia, near Haran

I. Shem-c1-1a.
Reu-Serug

Name	Translation	Age of Father	Other Info.
Serug (sē'rŭg)		Lived to age 230	Other sons and daughters
Nahor (nā' hôr)	Snorting	Serug 30 yrs.	

I. Shem-c1-1a.
Serug-Nahor(G)

Name	Translation	Age of Father	Other Info.
Nahor(G) (nā' hôr)Abram's **Grandfather***		Lived to age 148	Other sons and daughters;
Terah (tē'rȧ)	Station Terach (teh'-rakh)	Nahor 29 yrs.	

*(**G** = Grandfather of Abraham)

I. Shem-c1-a.
Nahor(G)-Terah-Wife-A

Name	Translation	Age of Father	Other Info.
Terah (tē'rȧ) A. wife undisclosed	Terach (teh'-rakh);	Lived to age 205	Didn't know God of his son Abraham
I. **Abram** (ā' brăm Abraham	Exalted father & high father	Terah 70 yrs. at son's birth	**Ancestor of Israel**

2. **Nahor** (nā' hôr) Abram's **Brother***	Snorting		named after his grandfather
3. **Haran** (hā' răn)	Mountaineer		**b**orn in Ur of the Chaldees, land of Haran; his daug. (Milcah) married his brother Nahor

*(**B** = Brother of Abraham; **G** = Grandfather of Abraham)*

I. Shem-c1-a.
Nahor(G)-Terah-Wife-B

Name	Translation	Age of Father	Other Info.
<u>Terah</u> (tē'rɑ́) **B.** wife undisclosed	Terach (teh'-rakh)	Lived to be 205	Father of Abram
Sarai (sâr' ɑ́)	Princess	Terah 70 yrs. old	Abram's half-sister; different mother

I. Shem-c1a-I.
Abram/Abraham-Hagar

Name	Translation	Age of Father	Other Info.
I. <u>**Abraham**</u> * (ā' brɑ́ hăm) & **Hagar** (hä·gär'_	Exalted father; Flight	Gen 16:16	Named Abraham (Gen 17:5); Hagar, maid of Sarah

| Ishmael (yish·mä·āl') | God hears | Abram 86 yrs. | Havilah-Shur, Egypt; Lived 137yrs. Gen 25:17 |

I. Shem-c1a-I.
Abram/Abraham-Sarai/Sarah

Name	Translation	Age of Father	Other Info.
I. **Abraham** * & **Sarai**	Father of multitude; Sarai a noblewoman	Gen 21:5 Gen 17:17	Father of Israel; Sarai to Sarah,(Gen 17:15)
II. **Isaac** *(ī' zȧk)	One laughs	Parents are 100 & 90	**Forefather of Israel**

I. Shem-c1a-II.
Abraham-Isaac

Name	Translation	Age of Father	Other Info.
II. **Isaac** * (ī' zȧk) & **Rebekah**	One laughs; Ensnarer	Gen 25:26	**Forefather of Israel**
a. Esau (ē'saw)	Hairy	Isaac 60 yrs.	Edom; Seir,
III. Jacob * (jȧ' kūb)	Supplanter, heel holder, deceitful	Ditto	**Name chg. to Israel; Father of Israel**

(God's Chosen; Gen 12:1-3; Gen 16:15-16; Gen 17:16-21)

~ Notes ~

[1] The King James Study Bible, Thomas Nelson Inc. 1988
[2] www.blueletterbible.org
[3] The New Compact Bible Dictionary, Zondervan Publishing House, 1967
[4] Unger's Bible Dictionary, Moody Press, 1981

Continuation of Shem (I) Family:

Nahor-B (Brother of Abraham), Haran, Lot, Bethuel, Laban, Rachel, Leah

Genesis 19:29-38; 25:19-26; 29:15-30; 30:1-25

I. Shem-c1a-2.
Terah-NahorB & Milcah

Name	Translation	Age of Father	Other Info.
2. NahorB* & **Milcah**	Snorting & queen/daug. of Haran		Brother of Abram & Haran;
a. Huz, (oots)	Wooded		
b. Buz, (booz)	Contempt		
c. Kemuel (kem-oo-ale)	Raised of God		
d. Chesed (keh'sed)	Increase		
e. Hazo, (khaz-o')	Vision		
f. Pildash (pil-dawsh')	Flame or fire		
g. Jidlaph (yid-lawf')	Weeping		
h. **Bethuel**, (beth-oo-ale')	Abode of God		Syrian; father of **Rebekah**,

I. Shem-c1a-2.
Terah-NahorB & Reumah

Name	Translation	Age of Father	Other Info.
2. NahorB* & Reumah	Snorting & elevated;		Gen 22:24; (reh-oo-maw')
a. Tebah	Slaughter		(teh'-bakh)
b. Gaham	Burning		(gah'-kham)
c. Thahash	Dugong		(takh'-ash)
d. Maachah	Oppression		(mah-ak-aw')

(B for Brother for brother of Abraham)

I. Shem-c1a-3.
Terah-Haran

Name	Translation	Age of Father	Other Info.
3. Haran * (hā' răn) & wife;	Mountaineer		Born in Ur; land of Haran; bro. of Abraham
a. Lot (lŏt)	Covering; envelope		Small bits of wood, pebble, in deciding an issue;
b. Milcah (daughter)	Queen; (mil-kaw')		Married her uncle, Nahor
c. Iscah (daughter)	One who looks forth(yis-kaw')		Gen 11:27-31

I. Shem-c1a-3a.
Terah-Haran-Lot

Name	Translation	Age of Father	Other Info.
a. **Lot** wife undisclosed	Covering; (lŏt)		Gen 19:30-38
daughter #1			
daughter #2			
These daughters made father drunk	Then slept with their father		Produced heirs; continued line of Lot
#1 begat Moab	Of his father		**Moabites**
#2 begat Ben-ammi	Son of my people		**Ammonites**

I. Shem-c1a-2h.
Of Peleg-Reu-Serug-Nahor-Terah
Bethuel

Name	Translation	Age of Father	Other Info.
2h. Bethuel (bë-thū' ël) & wife	Abode of God		Syrian of Padanaram
a. **Rebekah** * (rib-kaw')	Ensnarer		Sister of Laban, wife of Isaac,
b. **Laban,** Gen 24:29 (law-bawn')	White		Father of Leah & Rachel

(*More on Rebekah, pg.108)

I. Shem-c1a-2h-b.
Laban

Name	Translation	Age of Father	Other Info.
2. Laban & wife begat: Gen 29:16	White		Syrian of Padanaram
a. **Leah** * (lay-aw')	Weary, was soft & delicate		1st wife of Jacob; mother of Reuben, Simeon, Levi, Judah, Issachar, Zebulun, and Dinah
b. **Rachel** * (raw-khale)	Ewe, was beauty in looks and form		2nd wife of Jacob; mother of Joseph, and Benjamin

(*More on Leah and Rachel pgs. 109-111)

I. Shem-c1b.
Shem-(3)Arphaxad-Salah-Eber-Joktan

Name	Translation	Age of Father	Other Info.
b. <u>Joktan</u> (yok-tawn') 2nd son of Eber	Smallness		Patriarch of Arabia Shem's great-grand *Gen 10:26-32*
1. Almodad,	Not measured		(al-mo-dawd')
2. Sheleph	Drawing forth		(sheh'-lef)

3. Hazar-maveth (khats-ar-maw'-veth)	Village of death		So. Arabia
4. Jerah (yeh'-rakh)	New moon		Ancestor of Arabia
5. Hadoram	Noble honor		(had-o-rawm')
6. Uzal	Shall be flooded		(oo-zawl')
7. Diklah	Palm grove		(dik-law')
8. Obal	Stripped bare		(o-bawl')
9. Abimael	God (El) is my father		(ab-ee-maw-ale')
10. Sheba, (shev·ä')	Seven, (or oath)		Also name of a son of Cush,
11. Ophir, (o-feer')	Reducing to ashes		City of southern Arabia
12. Havilah (hăv' ĭ-lα) (khav-ee-law')	Sand land; circle		Pison river runs thru it
13. 13. Jobab (jō'băb)	Howler, calls loudly		Arabian descendants of Joktan;

I. Shem-cle.
Shem-Aram

Name	Translation	Age of Father	Other Info.
e. <u>**Aram**</u>* (ă'rɑm) *5th son of Shem*	Exalted, Syria		Aramaic, progenitor of Armenians
Uz (ŭz)	Wooded		The country of Job (Job 1:1); near Edom, Egypt, Moab, Philistia (Jer 25:20)
Hul (hŭl)	Circle		
Gether (gē-'thĕr)	Fear		
Mash (măsh) or Meshech	Drawn out		Meshech (mē'shĕk)

*(From page 94)

~ Notes ~

Continuation of Shem (I) Family:

Abram and Ishmael,
And
Abraham and Isaac, and Jacob

Genesis 16:1-16; 21:1-3;
25:19-26; 35:22-26

I. Shem Continued, Abraham-c1a-I.
Abraham's Son, Ishmael

Name	Translation	Age of Father	Other Info.
I. <u>Abraham</u> * (ā' brá hăm) & Hagar	Father of multitude; flight	Gen 16:16 Gen 17:5	Hagar, Sarah's Egyptian maid
a. **Ishmael** (ĭsh' mā-ĕl)	God hears	Abram age 86	Havilah, Shur, & Egypt near Assyria

(Continued from pg. 98)

I. Abraham's Son, Isaac-c1a-I.

Name	Translation	Age of Father	Other Info.
I. <u>Abraham</u> * & Sarah; sä·rä'	Father of a multitude; Noble woman	Gen 21:5 Gen 17:17	Forefather of Israel
II. **Isaac** *(ī' zák)	One laughs	Parents; 100/90	Father of Israel

I. Abraham, Isaac's Twin Sons-c1a-II.
Esau & Jacob

Name	Translation	Age of Father	Other Info.
II. Isaac (ĭ' zắk) & Rebekah	He laughs; ensnarer	Gen 25:20 & 26	Forefather of Israel
a. Esau (ē'saw)	Hairy,	Isaac age 60	Father of Arab people, & Edom
III. Jacob* (jă' kūb)	Supplanter/ deceitful or heel holder	Isaac age 60	Father of Israel

(God's Chosen to lead his people; Gen 12:1-3; Gen 16:15-16; Gen 17:16-21)

I. Shem, Abraham, Isaac, c1a-III.
Jacob's Sons (#s 1-4 & 9-10) & only Daughter
Born of Leah

Name	Translation	Age of Father	Other Info.
III. Jacob (jä' kūb) & Leah (lay-aw')	Supplanter; deceitful; heel holder; weary		Gen 29:31; & 30:24
1. Reuben (reh-oo-bane')	A son		Behold a son
2. Simeon (shim-one')	Heard		
3. Levi (lay-vee')	Attached or joined to		
4. Judah (yeh-hoo-daw')	Praise		Praise the Lord
9. Issachar (yis-saw-kawr')	Hire/Payment		
10. Zebulun (zeh-oo-loon')	Dwelling or Habitation		
* Dinah (dee-naw')	Judgment	Gen 34	Full sister to Simeon & Levi

I. Shem, Abraham, Isaac, c1a-III.
Jacob's Sons (#s 5-6)
Born of Rachel's Maidservant Bilhah

Name	Translation	Age of Father	Other Info.
III. Jacob (jă' kūb) & Bilhah (bil·hä')	Supplanter; deceitful; Bilhah-troubled		Gen 29:31; & 30:24
5. Dan (dawn)	Judge	Gen 34	
6. Naphtali (naf-taw-lee')	My Wrestlings		

I. Shem, Abraham, Isaac, c1a-III.
Jacob's Sons (#s 7-8)
Born of Leah's maidservant Zilpah (zil-paw')

Name	Translation	Age of Father	Other Info.
III. Jacob (jă' kūb) & Zilpah (zil-paw' or zil·pä	Supplanter; deceitful/heel holder; A trickling		Gen 29:31; & 30:24
7. Gad (gawd')	Troop or Fortune	Gen 30	
8. Asher (aw-share')	Happy		

I. Shem, Abraham, Isaac, c1a-III.
Jacob's Sons (#s 11-12)
Born of Rachel

Name	Translation	Age of Father	Other Info.
III. Jacob & **Rachel** raw'khale')	Ewe; tender eyed; beautiful	Gen 30:22	Israel
11. **Joseph** (yo-safe'/jŏ'zĕf)	He will add		
12. **Benoni** (ben·ō·nē') **Benjamin** (bin-yaw-mene')	Son of sorrow Son of Right Hand	Gen 35;16-18	

I. Shem, Abraham, Isaac, Jacob, Joseph, c1a-III-#11.
Joseph's Sons
Born to him in Egypt of daughter of Potiphar

Name	Translation	Age of Father	Other Info.
11. Joseph & Asenath (ä·se·nath' or aw-se-nath')	He will add; & of the goddess Neith		Gen. 41:46-53
1. **Manasseh** (men-ash-sheh')	Making Forgetful	30-37 yrs. at birth of sons	
2. **Ephraim** (ef-rah'-yim)	Fruitfulness		

~ Notes ~

Continuation of Shem (I) Family:

Abraham, Ishmael & Sons

Abraham, Keturah & Sons

Genesis 25:1-5, 12-18

I. Shem, Abram/Abraham-Hagar, Ishmael, c1a-Ia.
Ishmael's Sons

Name	Translation	Age of Father	Other Info.
a. **Ishmael** (ĭsh' mā-ĕl) & wife	God will hear		
Nebajoth (neb-aw-yoth')	Heights		Nabateans, Petra as capital
Kedar (kay-dawr')	Dark		
Adbeel (ad-beh-ale')	Chastened of God		
Mibsam (mib-sawm')	Sweet odour		
Mishma (mish-maw')	Hearing		
Dumah (doo'maw')	Silence		
Massa (mas-saw')	Burden		
Hadar/Hadad (khad-ar')	Honour		Also, an Edomite King
Tema (tay-maw')	Desert		
Jetur (yet-oor')	Enclosed		
Naphish (naw-feesh')	Refreshment		
Kedemah (kayd'-maw)	Original		
*Bashemath (bos-math')	spice	Gen 36:3	Daughter who married Esau

I. Shem, Abraham, c1a-I.
Abraham's Sons of Keturah

Name	Translation	Age of Father	Other Info.
I. **Abraham** (ā' brɑ hăm **Keturah** (ket-oo-raw')	Father of a multitude; incense		
1. Zimran (zim-rawn')	Musician		
2. *Jokshan (yok-shawn')	Snarer		
3. Medan (sheb-aw')	Contention		
4. *Midian (mid-yawn')	Strife		
5. Ishbak (yish-bawk')	He releases		Progenitor of Arabian tribe
6. Shuah (shoo'-akh)	Wealth		

I. Shem, Abraham, Keturah, c1a-I-2.
Sons of Jokshan

Name	Translation	Age of Father	Other Info.
2. Jokshan (yok-shawn')	Snarer		
a. Sheba (sheb-aw')	Seven or an oath		
b. **Dedan** (ded-awn')	Low country		

I. Shem, Abraham, Keturah, c1a-I-2b.
Sons of Dedan

Name	Translation	Age of Father	Other Info.
2b. <u>Dedan</u> & wife	Seven or an oath		
Asshurim (ash-shoo-ree')	Steps		
Letushim (let-oo-sheem')	Hammered		
Leummim (leh-oom-meem')	Peoples		

I. Shem, Abraham, Keturah, c1a-I-4.
Sons of Midian

Name	Translation	Age of Father	Other Info.
4. <u>Midian</u> (mid-yawn')& wife	Strife		Progenitor of Midianites or Arabians
a. Ephah ay-faw')	Gloomy		
b. Epher (ay'-fer)	A calf		
c. Hanoch or Enoch (khan-oke')	Dedicated		
d. Abidah or Abida (ab-ee-daw')	My father knows		
e. Eldaah (el-daw-aw')	God has known		

~ Notes ~

Continuation of Shem (I) Family:

Abraham, Isaac and Esau

Genesis 36

I. Shem, Abraham, Isaac, Esau: c1a-IIa.
Esau's Son of Wife Judith-1

Name	Translation	Age of Father	Other Info.
a. **Esau** (ā·säv') & **Judith** (yeh-ho-deeth')	Hairy; Jewess/praised	Gen. 26:34 Gen 36:9	Daughter of Beeri; Hittite of Canaan

I. Shem, Abraham, Isaac, Esau: c1a-IIa.
Esau's Son of Wife Adah-2

Name	Translation	Age of Father	Other Info.
a. **Esau** (ay-sawv') & **Adah** (aw-daw')	Hairy; Ornament	Gen 36:1-4	Daug. of Elon, Hittite of Canaan
2a. Eliphaz {el-ee-faz'}	My God is fine gold	Gen 36:10	

I. Shem, Abraham, Isaac, Esau: c1a-IIa.
Esau's Son of Wife Bashemath-3

Name	Translation	Age of Father	Other Info.
a. **Esau** (ay-sawv') & **Bashemath**	Hairy; Spice & (bos-math')	Gen 26:34	Daug. of Ishmael; sister of Nebajoth
3a. Reuel (reh-oo-ale')	Friend of God	Gen 36:1-4, 10	

I. Shem, Abraham, Isaac, Esau: c1a-IIa.
Esau's Son of Wife Mahalath-4

Name	Translation	Age of Father	Other Info.
a. **Esau** (ā·säv') & **Mahalath** (makh·al·ath')	Hairy; String instrument		Daughter of Ishmael Gen 28:9

I. Shem, Abraham, Isaac, Esau: c1a-IIa.
Esau's Sons of Wife Aholibamah-5

Name	Translation	Age of Father	Other Info.
a. **Esau** (ay-sawv') & **Aholibamah** (o'-hol-ee-baw-maw")	Hairy; & Tent of high place	Gen 36:5	Daughter of Anah; of Zibeon; Hivite of Canaan
5a. Jeush (yeh-eesh')	Assembler		Duke/Chief of Edom
5b. Jaalam (yah-lawm')	Concealed		Duke/Chief of Edom
5c. Korah (ko'rakh)	Bald		Duke/Chief of Edom

I. Shem, Abraham, Isaac, Esau: c1a-IIa-2a.
Grandsons of Eliphaz & Unnamed Wife, G1*

Name	Translation	Age of Father	Other Info.
2a. **Eliphaz** (el-ee-faz') & wife		Gen 36:10-11; 15-16	Gen 36:2, 15-16
G1a. Teman (tay-mawn')	South		Duke or Chief/ Edom;

G1b. Omar (o-mawr')	Speaker/ eloquent		Duke/Chief of Edom
G1c. Zepho (tsef-o')	Watch Tower		Duke/Chief of the Edomites
G1d. Gatam (gah-tawm')	A burnt valley		Duke/Chief of Edom
Kenaz (ken-az')	Hunter		Duke/Chief of Edom

(G is for Grandsons; G1=grandson of wife #1)

I. Shem, Abraham, Isaac, Esau: c1a-IIa-2a.
Grandsons of Eliphaz & Wife Timna, G2

Name	Translation	Age of Father	Other Info.
2a. Eliphaz (') & Timna,		Gen 36:12-16	Gen 36:12, 15-16
G2a. Amalek (am-aw-lake')	Valley dweller		Duke of Edom; ancestor of Amalekites

(G is for Grandsons; G2=grandson of wife #2)

I. Shem, Abraham, Isaac, Esau: c1a-IIa-2a.
Grandsons of Reuel & wife, G3

Name	Translation	Age of Father	Other Info.
3a. Reuel*(eh-oo-ale'); & wife		Gen 36:13, 17	Gen 36:4, 17
G3a. Nahath (nakh'-ath)	Rest		Duke/Chief of Edom;
G3b. Zerah (zeh'-rakh)	Rising		Duke/Chief of Edom

G3c. Shammah (sham-maw')	Astonishment		Duke/Chief of Edom
G3d. Mizzah (miz-zaw')	Fear		Duke/Chief of Edom

* Reuel, son of Bashemath, pg. 119; G3=grandson of Reuel's wife)

~ Notes ~

Continuation of Shem (I) Family:

Dukes of Esau,

Kings of Edom

The Horites,

Dukes of Seir

Genesis 36

Descendants of the Horites
Dukes of Seir-The Horite,
In the Land of Edom

Name	Translation	Age of Father	Other Info.
Seir (sē'ēr) (say-eer')	Hairy or Shaggy	Gen 14:6; 36:20-30	The Horite or Edom
1. **Lotan** (lo-tawn')	Covering or wrapping		
2. **Shobal** (sho-bawl')	Flowing		
3. **Zibeon** (tsib-one')	Hyena		
4. **Anah** (an-aw')	Answer		
5. **Dishon** (dee-shone')	Antelope or Thresher		
6. **Ezer** (ay'-tser)	Treasure		
7. **Dishan** (dee-shawn')	Almost same as Dishon		
8. Timna (tim-naw')	Restrained		Sister of Lotan, Gen 36:22

Sons of Duke Lotan (1)

Name	Translation	Age of Father	Other Info.
1. **Lotan;** (lō·tän')	Wrapping		Gen 36:20-22
Hori (kho-ree')	Cave Dweller		
Hemam/Homam (hay-mawm')	Exterminating		

Sons of Duke Shobal (2)

Name	Translation	Age of Father	Other Info.
2. **Shobal** (sho-bawl')	Flowing		Gen 36:23
Alvan/Alian (al-yawn')	Tall		
Manahath (maw-nakh'-ath)	Rest		
Ebal (ay-bawl')	Stone; bare mtn		
Shepho/Shephi (shef-o')	Bold		
Onam (o-nawm')	Vigorous		

Sons of Duke Zibeon (3)

Name	Translation	Age of Father	Other Info.
3. **Zibeon** (tsib-one')	Hyena		Gen 36:24
Ajah (ah-yaw')	Falcon		
Anah (an-aw')	Answer		Mules in Lev 19:19; Gen 36:24

Sons of Duke Anah (4)

Name	Translation	Age of Father	Other Info.
4. **Anah** (an-aw')	Answer	Gen 36:24-25	Gen 36:24
Dishon (dee-shone')	Antelope or Thresher		
Aholibamah, (o'-hol-ee-baw-maw')	Tent of high place		

Sons of Duke Dishon (5)

Name	Translation	Age of Father	Other Info.
5. **Dishon** (dee-shone')	Antelope or Thresher	Gen 36:24-26	
Hemdan/Amram (khem-dawn')	Pleasant or Desire		
Eshban (esh-bawn')	Man of understanding		

Ithran (yith-rawn')	Advantage		
Cheran (ker-awn')	Lyre		

Sons of Duke Ezer (6)

Name	Translation	Age of Father	Other Info.
6. **Ezer** (ay'-tser)	Treasure	Gen 36:27-30	
Bilhan (bil-hawn')	Foolish		
Zaavan (zah-av-awn')	Troubled		
Akan/Jaakan (aw-kawn')	Intelligent		

Sons of Duke Dishan (7)

Name	Translation	Age of Father	Other Info.
7. **Dishan** (dee-shawn')	Almost same as Dishon	Gen 36:28-30	
Uz (oots)	Wooded		
Aran (ar-awn')	Wild goat		

Dukes of Esau

Compare the following dukes of Esau/Edom of Genesis 36:40-43 with the dukes of Genesis 10-18.

Name	Translation	Age of Father	Other Info.
Esau (ay-sawv')	Hairy; Edom- Gen 36:43	Gen 36:40-43	Son of Isaac, brother of Jacob
1. Timnah (tim-naw')	Restraining		
2. Alvah/Aliah (al-vaw')	High or sublimity		
3. Jetheth (yeh-thayth')	Subjection		
4. Aholibamah (o'-hol-ee-baw-maw')	Tent of High Place		Same name as a wife of Esau
5. Elah (ay-law')	An oak		
6. Pinon (pee-none')	Darkness		
7. Kenaz (ken-az')	Hunter		
8. Teman (tay-mawn')	South		
9. Mibzar (mib-tsawr')	Fortress		
10. Magdiel (mag-dee-ale')	Prince of God		
11. Iram (ee-rawm')	Belonging to a city		

Kings of Edom, Gen 36:31-39

These kings ruled in the land of Edom, Before there were kings of Israel

I. Bela

Name	Translation	Age of Father	Other Info.
Bela (beh'-lah), Son of Beor	Swallowed Gen 36:31	Gen 36:32	Dinhabah, *(din-haw-baw')*

II. Jobab

Name	Translation	Age of Father	Other Info.
Jobab (yo-bawb'), Son of Zerah,	Shouting/trumpet call; (zeh'-rakh), Bold	Gen 36:33	Bozrah, (b o t s - r a w '); sheepfold/ fortress

III. Husham

Name	Translation	Age of Father	Other Info.
Husham (khoo-shawm')	Haste; Passion	Gen 36:34	Land of Temani; southward

IV. Hadad

Name	Translation	Age of Father	Other Info.
Hadad (had-ad'), Son of Bedad	M i g h t y ; Fierceness	Gen 36:34	Avith, (av-veeth'); ruins

V. Samlah

Name	Translation	Age of Father	Other Info.
Samlah (s a m-l a w')of Masrekah	A garment	Gen 36:36	Masrekah, or a vineyard of noble vines

VI. Saul

Name	Translation	Age of Father	Other Info.
Saul/Shaul (shaw-ool')	Asked of God; desired	Gen 36:37	Rehoboth, (rekh-o-voth'); wide places, by river.

VII. Baal-hanan

Name	Translation	Age of Father	Other Info.
Baal-hanan (bah'-al khaw-nawn'),	Baal is gracious	Gen 36:38	Son of Achbor, (ak-bore')

I. Hadar/Hadad

Name	Translation	Age of Father	Other Info.
Hadar/Hadad (had-ar') wife-Mehetabel, *(meh-hay-tab-ale';*	Honor	Gen 36:39	Pau/Pai, *(paw-oo'; bleating)*

~ Notes ~

Father of Twelve Tribes
Early Years
Genesis 25:26 - 27:45

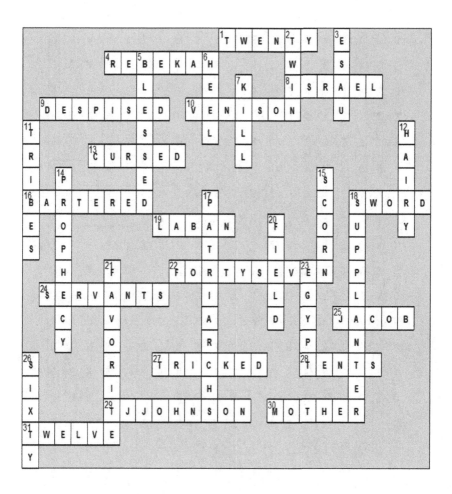

Created Using: Crossword Puzzle Maker

Blessings for Twelve Sons
Word Search Puzzle Answer Grid
Genesis 49

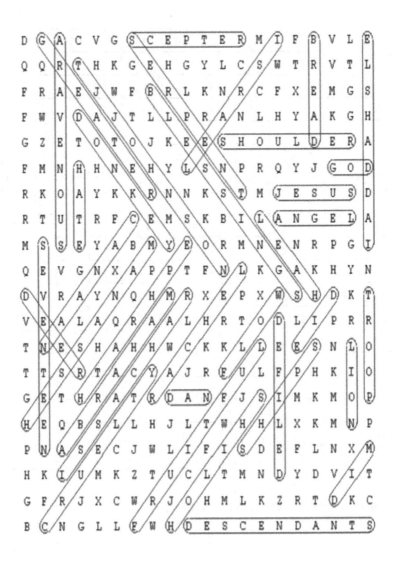

Constructed from: 1-2-3 Word Search ™

Canaan Dwellers Before Israel

https://www.blueletterbible.org/images/Joshua/imageDisplay/
tgb_022b[5]

~ Notes ~

[1] Unger's Bible Dictionary, Moody Press, 1981, pp 991
[2] The New Compact Bible Dictionary, Zondervan, 1967, pp 532
[3] www.blueletterbible.org
[4] Illustrated Davis Dictionary of The Bible, Royal Publishers, 1973
[5] Ibid, #3

~ THE END ~

Printed in the United States
By Bookmasters